PEEKS at the PEAK 2

Around and about the Peak District and Derbyshire near Sheffield
By Ann Beedham

Looking out from Longshaw

Contents

This is a second volume containing more of the popular and also not so well known places and people of the Peak District and its surrounds.

As well as the natural beauty of this part of the country, there are the tales and lives of the past inhabitants woven into its story. They left their mark too, along with the winds and rain; be it with the erection of fine buildings, being the catalyst for cultural or social change, or with the industrial remnants of their trades.

Today new generations live, work and spend their leisure time in and around the Peak District. They walk the same hills, have the same hopes and dreams.

The remnants of the past generations are beneath our feet, on the horizon or in the very evolution of the places we visit.

Perhaps as we stand gazing at the hills and edges today, our feet are on the same spot as a muscle weary Roman soldier, or a canal worker wandering home and breaking to catch his breath.

We are all part of the continuing story, the stream of people who pass through these places; places to enjoy, wonder at, treasure and respect.

Tideswell P1	Fanshawe Gate Hall P64
Clarion Ramblers P5	Bluebells P70
Renishaw Hall P6	Pentrich Revolution P71
Buxton the Spa P13	Cromford Canal P73
Lime burning P22	Cromford Mills P77
Florence Nightingale P25	Masson Mills P79
Lathkill Dale P28	William Gell P82
Peach of a Theatre P34	The Roundhouse P85
Bolsover Castle P37	Edith and the Sheik P91
Edale and Kinder Scout P45	Randolph Douglas P93
Hannah Mitchell P51	Poems P100
Wild Flowers P54	Bibliography/further reading P102
Dronfield Church P55	Useful Web sites etc P105
Edward Carpenter P58	Thanks to P106

This book is dedicated to the late Phil Eastwood of Grindleford Cafe, with thanks for the many happy hours spent in his characterful establishment, partaking of a milky coffee and mountainous chip buttie

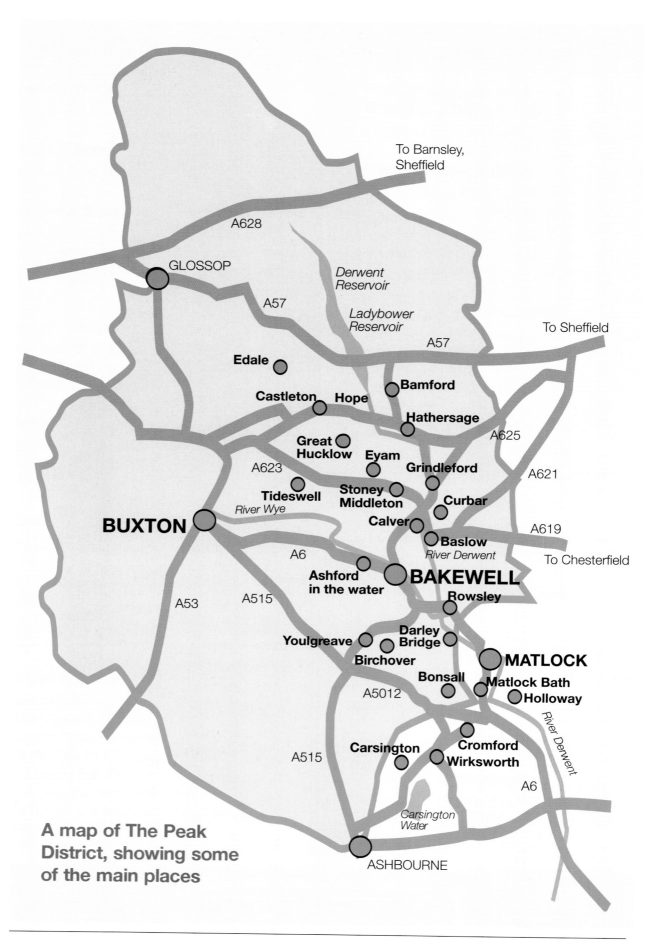

A map of The Peak District, showing some of the main places

Tideswell

St John the Baptist church at Tideswell is one of the largest in the area and is often called 'The Cathedral of the Peak.'

Known locally as 'Tidzer', Tideswell is one of the oldest settlements in the Peak District. At the time of the Domesday book of 1086 it was part of the Royal Manor of Hope. The main feature today is the beautiful 14th century church.

A historic place

In the year 1251, Tideswell was granted a market charter. It became a bustling and well known market place and grew prosperous through the trade of lead and wool. This is why the people there were able to afford such a grand church. Much of the building there was centred around the market place, but there is no longer a market.

Though it is a pretty place, with interesting shops and buildings, it is not as well frequented by tourists as other places in the Peak District.

Inside the 'Cathedral of the Peak'

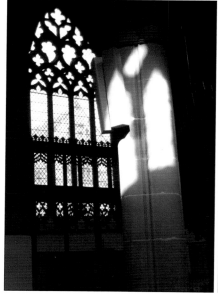

Some of the wooden screenwork

One of the windows

Boards of the ten commandments

The church of St John the Baptist is certainly impressive for its setting in a small community. There was probably a much smaller church on the site originally. Some traces of a Norman church can be seen in the chancel of the present church, which was started around 1300.

As the church was built, different styles from different periods were used. Some parts are in the Late Gothic style, some parts are closer to Perpendicular style, for example. The building was mainly funded by the Foljambe and Meverell families. There has been restoration work to the church but very little if any additions to the building itself since it was finished in 1400.

The Black Death delayed the building work and the lovely pinnacled tower and the west window were the last to be built.

Tideswell has an annual well dressing which starts on the saturday nearest the 24th of June, which is St John the Baptist's Day. Tideswell Wakes is also on at the same time.

Some of the fine carving to be seen

A 14th century bell in the church

The font at harvest time

The old door of the church

2

Some of the features

■ **WOOD CARVING** - Much of the carving in the church is by a man called Advent Hunstone, who lived in Tideswell. He made the lectern, the screen and the organ case, amongst many other pieces. His children carried on the crafts tradition in the village for three generations.

■ **SEDILIA-** This row of three seats with elaborate arches is seating for the clergy when they are taking a service.

■ **SCREEN-** This separates the Nave from the Chancel and is thought to be the oldest woodcarving work in the church

■ **TOMBS -**There are some fine old tombs in the church, including that of of Sir Meverill, a local knight who died in 1462. It was restored in 1875.

An older tomb is that of John Foljambe who died in 1358.

There are lovely, evocative alabaster carvings on the 14th century tomb of Sir Thurstan de bower and his wife. Note the fine detail on the clothes and on the wife's striking head dress.

Sir Thurstan has his feet resting on a rather smiley lion, which symbolises his courage in battle.

■ **BRASSES** - There are some fine brasses, including ones to Sir John Foljambe and one to Bishop Robert Pursglove. It was the bishop who founded a grammar school here in 1560.

■ **MISERICORDS-** These are tip up seats, the underside of which are filled with lovely carvings. They were for people to rest on during long services. Resting like this they could look as if they were still standing up.

The tomb of John Foljambe, who died in 1358

The tomb of Sir Thurstan de Bower and his wife The lion is in a circle

The church exterior

Grave of a 'minstrel'

In the churchyard is the tomb of William Newton, 'Minstrel of the Peak' who died in 1830 aged 80. It was the writer and poet Anna Seward, daughter of an Eyam clergyman who christened him the 'minstrel of the Peak.'

Newton was born into a humble family in Abney, Derbyshire and taught himself how to write. He was trained as a carpenter but wanted to be a poet. He met Anna Seward, who encouraged him in his work.

Newton moved to Tideswell and became the manager of nearby Cressbrook Mill. Life at the mill was hard for the workers, many of them children. Children were sent from workhouses in other parts of the country to be employed at the mill. They endured long hours and a meagre diet to fortify their hard labours.

The grave of William Newton, 'Minstrel of the Peak'

Grammar School

Bishop Robert Pursglove founded the grammar school here in 1560. It closed in 1927 and is now home for the local library.

Sundial

There is a sundial in the churchyard, The base on which this stands is likely to be that of an old churchyard cross.

The door of the church

The sundial

Left, the old Grammar School, now a library and information centre

Buildings at the rear of the church

Clarion Ramblers

One of the best known local rambling groups the Sheffield Clarion Ramblers was formed in 1900 by a man called G.H.B Ward

"A Rambler made is a man improved!" So says the motto on the front of the pocket sized handbooks of the Sheffield Clarion Ramblers.

Escaping the city

In 1900, the clear air and beauty of the Peak District was a great perk to workers after a week of hard slog in the dirty, dusty and dangerous conditions of many of the trades of Sheffield. Droves went out on a Sunday, the only day off for most, rambling the hills and clearing the lungs of city smog.

Rambling was free and so a popular activity with the working class who could take part no matter how empty the pocket. The rambling groups had many members drawn from Communist or Socialist groups and so these groups became a sort of focus for working class social movement.

The hills the groups walked were often restricted, as some areas were owned by landed gentry and access was not allowed. Ramblers such as the Clarion groups were a challenge to these limitations and became a means of organising protest, lobbying and campaigning for access rights.

One man who was a champion of these rights was a Sheffield engineer called George Herbert Bridges Ward. It was he who founded the Sheffield Clarion Ramblers group in 1900. Ward claimed it was the first active rambling club of its kind to be formed in Britain.

In the first Sunday in September of that year the group had their first walk - on Kinder, later the scene for the famous mass trespass of 1932.

By 1910, Ward had started producing the Sheffield Clarion Ramblers' handbook, a pocket sized book crammed with information and walks and still prized today. These handbooks educated the reader about wildlife, history and many other subjects and had anecdotes, poetry and songs too.

As GHB Ward says in one of the handbooks, they "began with 4 pages of abbreviated ramble routes, tea places, notes on points of interest and two quotations from Wordsworth."

The handbook for 1951, the year the Peak District National Park was formed

SHEFFIELD CLARION RAMBLERS
1951-52
Fifty-first Year
Price 2/-
A Rambler made is a man improved !

Bakewell Church, Cottages, and Electric Standard, or, Ancient and Modern. Photo by Miss B. Dyson.
The man who never was lost, never went very far

Ward continued as Editor of these handbooks for 47 years and still found time to write lots of other things too and take part in many activities to further his cause.

Ever campaigning and protecting the rights of the rambler, Ward formed the Hallamshire Footpath Preservation Society in 1912. He was also instrumental in forming what is now called The Ramblers' Association.

After retiring from his steelworks job Ward could spend more time in the outdoors, He lived on Moorwoods Lane at Owler Bar, a good spot to be able to do so.

Ward died in 1957, but the efforts and energy he put into his life live on for all the people who benefit from walking the countryside.

It was Ward and people like him that were instrumental in leading the way for the creation of the Peak District National Park in 1951. The handbook for 1951-52, the fifty first year, was therefore a specially poignant one, the 50th annual handbook and the first year of the new Peak National Park.

It begins with an introduction by GHB Ward, ending in the words: "now we'll sing "A Jovial Tramp Am I" Then follows the song lyrics, with a chorus of

"a climbing tramp is a blessed scamp,
And a merry dog when he's very damp."

Also in this edition for the walk on June 24th, midsummer's day, is a poem 'Lines to our first National Park' by C P Wells which is dedicated to GHB Ward 'in appreciative gratitude.' An extract from the poem is below

"Joyous are we of the rambling fraternity that
Peakland is ours from now for eternity.

And, grateful and humble, we thank those who fought
For our generation may see what they wrought."...

"So then shall the Peak District National Park
Be used for our pleasure from dawn until dark
Be used as a treasure - a heritage grand!
A boon and a blessing to all in our land."

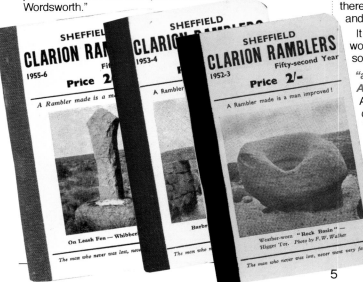

SHEFFIELD CLARION RAMBLERS 1955-6 Price 2/- A Rambler made is a m...
On Leash Fen — Whibber...
The man who never was lost, nev...

SHEFFIELD CLARION RAMBLERS 1953-4 A Rambler...
Barb...
The man who...

SHEFFIELD CLARION RAMBLERS 1952-3 Fifty-second Year Price 2/- A Rambler made is a man improved !
Weather-worn "Rock Basin" — Higger Tor. Photo by F.W. Walker
The man who never was lost, never went very far

The Gothic temple beneath a canopy of sunlit trees

Renishaw Hall

This picturesque hall, with beautiful gardens, is the home of the famous, literary Sitwell family

Renishaw Hall, viewed from the gardens

Enchantment seems to hang over this lovely place, a kind of otherworldly timelessness, where the hum of bees and scent of roses seems to have been going on forever. But it is not a place that stands still, with new additions and events always adding to the special ambience that pervades Renishaw Hall and Gardens.

The first hall

The Sitwell family first became connected to Renishaw in 1625, when the first George Sitwell acquired the land and built the first manor house on the site. This original hall now forms the three storeyed centre of the present one.

SHEFFIELD
M1
32
31
A57
MOSBOROUGH
M1
A625
A61
A616
Renishaw Hall
B6054
ECKINGTON
30
A619
N
A619

A work of art

After the first Sir George had begun the work on the gardens, they developed until 1797. It was then that they were redesigned in the style of Capability Brown, a popular trend at the time, which involved getting rid of much of the previous work and leaving hardly any garden at all.

The gardens at Renishaw were created by Sir George Sitwell, fourth Baronet and grandfather of the present owner Sir Reresby, between 1886 and 1938. He went back to the original style of 1625, with statues and water features.

The present owners Sir Reresby and Lady Sitwell, who took over the hall in 1965, from Sir Osbert Sitwell, have added their own ideas and efforts to the gardens, enhancing them greatly.

Today, as you visit, it almost as if you are discovering a huge secret garden, for the entrance is through a narrow path in a shrubbery, which opens into a wonderful view.

There are expansive lawns, sculptured yew pyramids and hedges and flower borders planted in the English tradition bursting with colour and variety. On a warm day the scent of roses hangs in the air and sun dappled woodland areas tempt exploration, There is a fine pond topped with waterlilies, a pool with a fountain to shed rainbows in the sun and statues that gaze serenely over the vistas.

The old hall in the picture book garden

A few of the features in the gardens

Gothic temple

One of the first things you see as you walk into the gardens is the gothic temple on the right, a round, castellated structure with elegant arches. This was built in 1808 as a conservatory by Sir Sitwell Sitwell. It has also been used as an aviary and now has become a cemetery to lay to rest the family's pet dogs.

The 'candles'

As you descend from the top lawn into the rest of the garden there is a white fountain before you. It is made of marble from a quarry near Verona, Italy. This, and one opposite to it at the other side of the lawn, are called the candles, as they look a little like elaborate candle holders. There are open mouthed fountain heads in the form of faces.

A face from one of the 'candles'

The swimming pool and fish pond

This Swimming Pool Garden is one of the three rose gardens, along with the First Candle and Second Candle gardens. At its centre is a swimming pool, with a fountain. This was the first feature Sir Reresby added to the gardens.

The lily decked fish pond was the last area of the garden to be created by Sir George. At its centre is an 'island' reached by a short causeway, which has yew ramparts enclosing fine shrubs.

Diana and Neptune

If you stand in front of the hall and look along the gardens. there are two statues in front of you, one on each side of the steps, which are also looking out to the view of the countryside beyond.

On the left is the goddess Diana, with her hound at her heels. On the right is Neptune, looking as if he has just been for a quick dip in the pool, as he is drying himself with a stone bath towel. These are by a sculptor named Caligari.

A rescued stone tank

In the stone tank garden, by the side of the woodland, is the feature that gives the area its name. The tank was found in a field on the estate and is now planted with papyrus which was brought back from the Nile by the Sitwell family.

The border around it is filled with dramatic foliage plants, including the giant Gunnera anicata, which looks like enormous elephants ears.

The statues of Diana and Neptune

A living natural art gallery

The 'Ha-Ha' wall

An array of plants

Walking around the gardens, beneath and around the wealth of beautiful trees, there is a wonderful array of colours, shapes and textures. Each corner holds another delight for the eye and nose.

The walls of the hall lend themselves as home to Wisteria, Jasmine, Honeysuckle, Ceanothus which, in summer, perfume the patio below. The ballroom, to the right in the picture on the right, is planted in a colour scheme of blue, yellow and white. Plants include Gentian, Monkshood, Delphiniums, lupins, sunflower and iris.

Around the garden with the first 'candle' are over a hundred types of roses, edged with box. Shrubs grow along with the roses, as is the tradition in the garden. Many more rare and unusual roses can be seen in the swimming pool garden.

One of Renishaw's trademark plants is the Scottish Flame Flower, which grows up to ten feet a season and produces scarlet flowers from june to September.

The bottom terrace is home to the hottest and driest border. The planting here is less formal and includes fuchsias, Ceanothus and a Rhododendron named after Dame Edith Sitwell.

At the front of the garden, which is farthest from the hall, is the National Yucca Collection. There are over 30 species of Yucca in the collection

The hot dry border they are in is hidden from the rest of the garden by the 'ha-ha' wall. This is a type of wall, which fools people looking along the view into thinking that there is no change in level, when in fact there is. They are used to keep sheep and cattle from the gardens.

Two statues of giants share the Half Moon borders and beyond is a view of the parkland and lakes.

The vineyard

One of Sir Reresby's interests is the wine trade and in 1972, he planted the vineyard at Renishaw Hall. It was created on the old Top Paddock, where Sir Sitwell Sitwell used to exercise his horses and for many years was the most northerly vineyard in Europe.

Colour and beauty in the borders

Woods and wilderness

Entrance to the Wilderness, with the statues Warrior and Amazon as sentries

The Classical Temple

The Wilderness

After wandering in the idyllic gardens, there is a wilderness to explore too. The 'gateway to the wilderness' subject of an evocative and lovely painting by John Piper, is flanked by two jaunty looking statues, Warrior and Amazon.

A classical temple can be found as you walk beneath the trees, In spring it is surrounded by a wonderful carpet of bluebells.

The Laburnum Tunnel

The New Woodland Garden was developed in 2001. Many other rare tree and shrubs were added to the site and the Holly hedge was lengthened. A shady Laburnum tunnel was also created.

The Laburnum tunnel

The lakes

Swans by the lake

Sir George Sitwell wanted a focal point for the areas beyond the main garden, with view beyond view as a kind of natural art gallery. He liked the idea of a shimmering lake to add to this gallery:

"The garden must be considered not as a thing by itself but as a gallery of foregrounds designed to set off the soft hues of the distance, it is nature which should call the tune and the melody is to be found in the prospect of blue hill or shimmering lake."

From Sir George's essay On The Making Of Gardens

Two main lakes were excavated in 1892, by unemployed fishermen from Scarborough. A third lake was made in 2000, by one man and a mechanical digger.

As well as adding beauty to the estate, the lakes also had a practical use. Water was pumped up from a small Victorian power station next to the lake and used as a domestic supply.

The old Pump House

The old pump house, with a tall red brick chimney, us still standing. It was adapted for use as a sawmill. The sawmill was first driven by a turbine, then by steam and finally by an engine.

Acquired during the Second World War, this engine, a Ruston's stationary engine had been commissioned by the Tsar before the First World War in 1914.

The engine, named Lizzie, can be seen in the second stable yard.

Lizzie

The lovely sun dappled woodlands at Renishaw

A Literary Dynasty

For almost 400 years, the Sitwell family have resided at Renishaw Hall. Many people are familiar with the Sitwell name because of the fame of some of the more recent members of the family, who were all writers.

The Sitwell family were first mentioned in the area as far back as the early 14th century, but the first of the family to be described as 'of Renishaw', was George Sitwell, born in 1600. He inherited early family fortunes and lands built up from the ownership of coal mines. George built the first manor house on the site, the central part of the present hall, in 1625. He consolidated the family wealth with profits from an iron works he started, which was prolific in its output of iron nails.

The succession of ownership is explained fully in a book on sale at Renishaw, written by Sir Reresby Sitwell.

It was Sir George Reresby Sitwell, the present Sir Reresby's grandfather, who was father to the trio of literary children, Edith, Osbert and Sacheverell.

Sir George had a passion for an Italian castle he bought, in Tuscany. He spent a lot of time, money and energy restoring it and eventually he and his wife went to live there.

It was his son Osbert who then took over the estate at Renishaw, settling there in the 1920s. Sacheverell ("Sachie") lived at a smaller family house, Weston, in Northamptonshire.

Osbert and his sister Edith were well known, if somewhat eccentric personalities and made many tours of England and the United States.

In later life, Osbert sadly developed Parkinson's Disease and so gave over the house and family estates at Renishaw to his elder nephew, Sir Reresby.

There is a fascinating Museum of Sitwell Memorabilia at the hall, with many family items, books and photographs on display.

The jockey painted in Sir Sitwell's colours

The Stables and Courtyards

The archway leading into the stables and courtyards. Inset: A dove cote in the first courtyard

The fine classical style stables were built in 1795. The jockey weathervane atop the stables entrance clocktower is painted in the colours green with an orange cap. These were the colours recorded for Sir Sitwell Sitwell in 1810 and still held by his descendants.

There is a Gallery Cafe for refreshments to visitors of the hall and gardens and the John Piper Gallery (see below).

Exhibitions and viewings

Apart from the family museum there is a Performing Arts gallery which houses various exhibitions throughout the year, such as theatrical costumes, ballet costumes and paintings and The Costume Gallery.

Another delight is the John Piper Gallery, with a different selection on show each year. John Piper's lively and atmospheric paintings and stained glass are very well known and sought after. Renishaw Hall was a favourite subject. Piper also illustrated Osbert Sitwell's autobiography, Left Hand, Right Hand.

There is also a Children's Adventure Garden with a maze, stoytelling bower, a living willow tunnel and a Tree Trail.

Tours and events

Throughout the year Renishaw holds some interesting events, such as open air theatre, and weekends with the themes of food and farming, art and crafts and World War Two.

Tours of the gardens, vineyard and the interior ground floor of the hall are available for booking. Tours of the interior are for groups of 25 - 50.

The hall is also available for civil weddings, which are held in the 18th century Red Dining Room and conferences, held in a room in the 18th century stable block.

■ Renishaw Hall, Renishaw, S21 3WB
■ Telephone: 01246 432310
■ Website: www.sitwell.co.uk

Buxton the spa

This is an elegant place, with festivals, grand pavilions, an Opera House and stylish shops

Buxton is a grand place, with a crescent based on that of Bath, a fabulous opera house and many other fine buildings which betray its affluent past as a spa destination for those in search of 'the cure'.

Healing waters

Long before the Georgians, Edwardians and Victorians came in droves to sample the delights and waters of the inland resort of Buxton, the Romans had discovered the warm springs, which are at a constant 28 degrees centigrade. It must have been a perk for them to bathe there, warming themselves against the English winter, at 1,300ft above sea level. The Romans established a settlement, calling it Aquae Arnemetiae "The Waters of the Goddess of the Grove". It became an important Roman site, like the other well known spa town Bath "Aquae Sulis").

After the Romans left, the place we now know as Buxton became forgotten. There was a shrine to St Anne, built around 1200, but it was really in Queen Elizabeth's reign that the place began to get popular again.

The captive queen's hall

The famous and ill fated Royal, Mary, Queen of Scots, under the custodianship of the 6th Earl of Shrewsbury, was allowed to visit the town's spa waters to try and help her rheumatism.

A hall, now turned into the Old Hall Hotel, was specially built to house her visits, under house arrest.

It was Built by Bess of Hardwick and her husband George Talbot, the 6th Earl of Shrewsbury, Mary's captor, on the site of an even earlier hall. It is the oldest building in Buxton, dating back to about 1570 in parts.

Many other prominent Elizabethans visited Mary and Buxton and it became a fashionable spot for the wealthy.

A room on the first floor of the hotel is still called the Scots Room. In one of the bedrooms there is a poem, 'Farewell to Buxton' scratched on the window pane. It is reputed to have been scratched by Mary herself, with her diamond ring, *"Buxton, whose fame thy milkwarm waters tell, whom I perhaps shall see no more, farewell"*.

If these are Mary's words they proved true, as after this she became involved with a plot to overthrow Queen Elizabeth, The Babington Plot. Elizabeth had Mary and her co her co-conspirators executed.

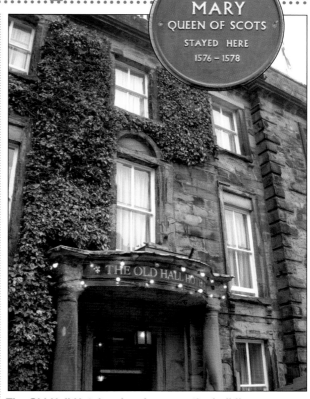

The Old Hall Hotel and a plaque on the building

The Duke of Devonshire rebuilt the hall in 1670, but some of the Shrewsbury's hall is hidden behind the facade of the new one.

The writer Daniel Defoe visited Buxton, during his 'Tour through the Whole Island of Great Britain' in the 18th century, and seemed quite impressed with his stay....

"The Duke of Devonshire is lord of the village, and consequently of the bath itself; and his grace has built a large handsome house at the bath, where there is convenient lodging, and very good provisions, and an ordinary well served for one shilling per head..."

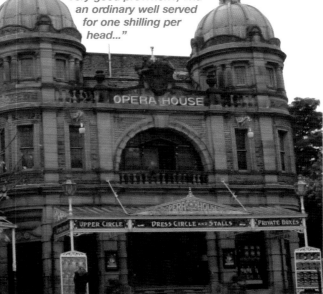

Buxton Opera House

A look at the town

The Crescent

The medicinal properties of the waters became recognised as one of the 'Seven Wonders of the Peak', and their fame grew throughout the 17th and 18th Centuries. With many people wanting to visit and needing accommodation, the 5th Duke of Devonshire was inspired to provide The Crescent (1784), for the benefit of wealthy visitors. The builder was John Carr of York.

The crescent was inspired by that at the other famous spa town, Bath. It is currently being restored as a spa hotel.

St. Ann's Well

Opposite the Crescent stands St Ann's Well, built over the natural spring. People can often be seen filling up their bottles with the warm spring waters that flow from it. This well was presented to the town in 1940 and the basin bears the words 'A well of living waters'.

Left: The well, above, the well head and below, the inscription

The Pump Room

Adjacent to the well is the Pump Room. This was built in 1894 and visitors came here to relax and take the water, which collected in a white marble well. The building was designed by Henry Currey. The building used to have two domes, but they were removed around the 1930s.

It was used to take the waters until 1981, after which it was briefly converted into a Micrarium. It is at time of writing uses as an art gallery exhibition space and awaiting redevelopment

The Pump Room and the interior, with a plaque that is found on the wall there

A look at the town

A literary dip

Daniel Defoe, (author of Robinson Crusoe) tried the delights of Buxton waters on his travels, during his search for 'The Seven Wonders Of The Peak.' He seemed to be quite taken with the healing properties of the spa and with the bathing!:

"Though I shall not treat this warm spring as a wonder, for such it is not; I must nevertheless give it the praise due to the medicinal virtues of its waters; for it is not to be deny'd, but that wonderful cures have been wrought by them, especially in rheumatick, scorbutick and scrofulous distempers, aches of the joints, nervous pains and also in scurfy and leprous maladies."

"The waters are temperately hot, or rather warm, and operate rather as a cold bath, but without that violent attack which the cold bath makes upon all nature at once; you feel a little chillness when you first dip or plunge into the water, but it is gone in a moment; and you find a kind of an quality in the warmth of your blood and that of the water, and that so very pleasant, that far from the fainting and weakening violence of the hot baths, which make you ready to die away if you continue above an hour, or thereabouts, in them, and will shrivel up the fingers like those of women, who have been washing cloathes; on the contrary, here you are never tired, and can hardly be persuaded to come out of the bath when you are in."

The old baths, now the Tourist Information Centre

There is a wonderful row of canopied shops in Buxton

The Slopes

This lovely green space at the heart of Buxton was used as an exercise area by those taking 'the cure'. Originally called St Ann's Cliff, it became known as The Slopes. The area was laid out in 1818 by Sir Jeffrey Wyatville but remodelled by Joseph Paxton in 1840. Elegant urns add more grandeur..

Museum and Art Gallery

This is sited in an old hotel, with fine stained glass and has many interesting collections, including that of Randolph Douglas and his House of Wonders from Castleton, described elsewhere in this book.It was opened by William Boyd Dawkins, a natural historian and cave hunter, whose recreated study now forms one of the rooms in the museum.
■ Buxton Museum & Art Gallery
Terrace Road, Buxton. Tel: 01298 24658
e mail: buxton.museum@derbyshire.gov.uk

Tourist Information Centre

Originally built by Henry Currey, in 1851, as a bathing place on the site of the spring which Mary Queen of Scots would have used. It opened as the town baths in 1924, and was used until 1972 when new pool was built in the Pavilion Gardens. It is now the Tourist Information Centre.

Also in the building you can see the Buxton Mineral Water being pumped from the spring for commercial sale, along with an interesting display .
■ Tourist Information Centre, The Crescent Buxton
■ Tel: 01298 25106 ■ email: tourism@highpeak.gov.uk
www.visitbuxton.co.uk

Cavendish Arcade

A stylish shopping arcade now makes good use of the old hot or thermal baths which were built by Currey in 1854. Some old features can still be seen, including fine Minton tiles and a chair and lift into a plunge bath. The original roof was in the ridge and furrow method, designed by Joseph Paxton and used on his glass houses at Chatsworth and later on the Crystal Palace. The building was re-developed in 1987 as the Cavendish arcade. There is now a stained glass barrel vaulted roof, by artist Brian Clark.
www.cavendisharcade.com

The Cavendish Arcade, with glass roof, Minton tiling and old plunge pool

A stable that became a hospital

The impressive dome, built over the old exercise yard

Signs for the well and pump from the hospital

The huged domed building seen on higher ground behind the crescent was built in 1785. It was originally stabling for The Crescent, with a circular colonnaded courtyard for exercising the horses and accommodation for the grooms.

In 1859 it was converted into the Devonshire Royal Hospital for the sick poor, supported by the Buxton Baths Charity.

The poor were kept far away from the richer visitors taking the waters elsewhere in the town, with their own spa water supply (see right). They took exercise in the hospital grounds.

The central exercise yard they used was covered over by a splendid domed roof, in 1881-82. This dome was, and still is, a great engineering feat and remains one of the largest unsupported domes in the country. At the time it was built, it was said to be the largest unsupported dome in the world.

The novelist Vera Britten, who once lived in Buxton, worked at the hospital for a while during the First World War and gives us a description of the place, in her novel Testament of Youth:

"On Sunday morning, June 27th 1915, I began my nursing at the Devonshire Hospital........
"The hospital had originally been used as a riding-school, but a certain Duke of Devonshire, with exemplary concern for the welfare of the sick but none whatever for the feet of the nursing staff, had caused it to be

converted to its present charitable purpose. The main part of the building consisted of a huge dome, with two stone corridors running one above the other round its quarter mile circumference. As kitchens, sink-rooms and wards all led off the circular corridors and appeared to have been built as far from one another as possible, the continuous walking along the unresistant stone floors must have amounted, apart from the work itself, to several miles a day."

The University of Derby now occupies the site.

Near the Devonshire Hospital Drinking Well is The Old Court House, now a stylish shopping arcade. This has vaulted ceilings and walls 3ft thick. Look out for the carved faces on the frontage, (one of which is pictured left).

Vera Brittain (1893-1970)

Vera Brittain is best known for her book 'Testament of Youth' and the popular television series which was based on it. She was also a very active campaigner for the peace movement, to which she had a lifelong commitment.

The Brittain family lived in Buxton, though Vera didn't seem too impressed with the place or the people of the time, as these quotes from Testament of Youth demonstrate:

"When I was eleven our adored governess departed, and my family moved from Macclesfield to a tall grey stone house in Buxton, the Derbyshire "mountain spa.

"I cannot remember that anyone ever came to the house of more interest to me than relatives, or mentally restricted local residents with their even more limited wives.

These families were typical of the kind that still inhabit small country towns; the wives "kept house" and the husbands occupied themselves as branch bank-managers, cautious and unenterprising solicitors, modest business men who preferred safety to experiment and 'family' doctors whose bedside manner camouflaged their diagnostical uncertainties."

"Buxton, which my father used to describe as "a little box of social strife lying at the bottom of a basin," must have had a population of about twelve thousand apart from the visitors who came to take the waters.

"Even at eighteen, a mentally voracious young woman cannot live entirely upon scenery."

"At my first dance, The High Peak Hunt Ball, I appeared modestly attired in the conventional white satin and pearls; this ingenious uniform entitled me to spend the greater part of the next few weeks gyrating to the strains of "Dreaming" and "The Vison of Salome" in the arms of physically boisterous and conversationally inept young men".

Later in life Vera studied at Somerville College Oxford. In 1923 she published her first novel, 'The Dark Tide'. It was an account of life in Oxford and the sexism she encountered.

'Testament of Youth', (1933), tells the story of how she left Oxford to train as a nursing auxiliary, and how she went on to nurse wounded soldiers during the first World War. Many people Vera cared for, including her brother, her husband to be and several close friends were killed in the conflict.

The book was based on her diary, which she began in 1913.

After the war she worked as a teacher in Oxford and in 1922 moved to London. She also travelled and wrote her novels.

When the Second World War began she was active in many anti war campaigns, such as that against 'saturation bombing' and from 1940 to 1946, she produced her fortnightly 'Letter to Peace-lovers', which gained 2,000 subscribers.

Vera carried on with peace work all her life, supporting such projects as the Campaign for Nuclear Disarmament.

'Testament of Experience', a novel in which Vera describes her life and her work for peace, was published in 1957.

Higher Buxton

Walking up The Slopes leads to what was the original town centre before the Crescent was built. There has been a market held in the square here for almost 200 years, the highest market in England.

The square is dominated by the Town Hall, built in 1889. This once held the museum. In front of the Town Hall stand remains of an old cross, thought to date from the 15th century, and set on a plinth. It may have once been a preaching cross, or a wayfarer cross, giving directions to travellers, and used to stand near the Palace Hotel.

The square is also home to a parade of shops known as The Eagle Parade, named after the Eagle Hotel, an old coaching inn on the London to Glasgow route and built around 1760.

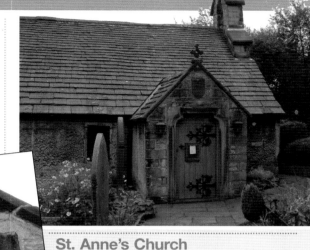

The old cross in the market square

The date on St Anne's church

St. Anne's Church

This quaint, unusual looking chapel sized church dedicated to St Anne is on Bath Road, not far from the market place. It dates dates from 1625 and was used as a school after a new church was opened. It is one of the oldest buildings in the town.

The Pavilion Gardens

The Pavilion Buildings

The Octagon, from the bandstand

These lovely gardens and the Pavilion Buildings date from 1871. A seven-year restoration project was completed in 2004 and they are now back to the original Victorian style and grandeur. There are 23 acres of walks and lakes for people to enjoy, like the generations before them. There are places to eat, and the Octagon building houses many events and fairs, including popular antique fairs. A bandstand now further enhances the gardens.

■ Pavilion gardens, St Johns Road, Buxton 01298 23114
■ email: paviliongardens@highpeak.gov.uk
■ www.paviliongardens.co.uk

This sign can be seen by a road near the gardens

Ducks Crossing

Broad walk, which runs along the side of the gardens was designed by Paxton in the 1860s. It was originally known as Cavendish Terrace after the Duke of Devonshire's family, as he financed its building

The Opera House

One of the gems of the Peak District, this lovely Opera House was thankfully rescued and restored in 1980.

It was built in 1903 by theatre architect Frank Matcham in grand Edwardian style.

Just over twenty years later it was converted into a cinema. Following a period when it had fallen into disuse.

After being restored and re-opened as an opera house, it is now a premier venue for music, theatre, comedy and dance. It is also the home of the annual Gilbert and Sullivan Festival and Puppet Festival.

FESTIVAL AND EVENT DATES:
■ March: Peak District Walking Festival
■ May: Antiques Fair
■ July: Buxton Festival, Festival Fringe, Puppet Festival, Buxton Well Dressings & Carnival Procession
■ August: International Gilbert & Sullivan Festival

The splendid Buxton Opera House

A putti from the Opera House interior

At the side of the nearby Opera House is a Conservatory, a lovely lush and exotic oasis of native and tropical plants

The elegant, colonnaded Square opposite the Opera House was built in 1802-3, as upmarket accommodation

This old post box of 1867 is across from the Opera House. It is a rare example and bears the monogram VR

18

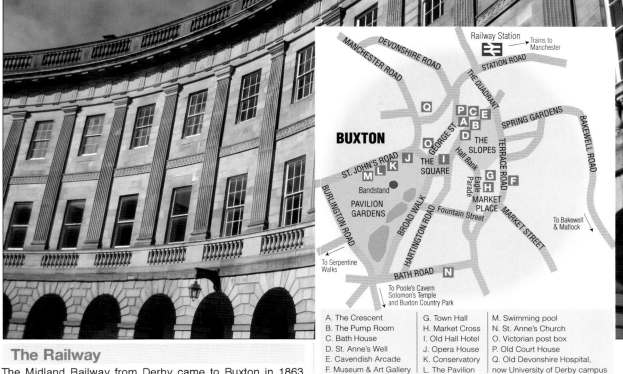

BUXTON

A. The Crescent	G. Town Hall	M. Swimming pool
B. The Pump Room	H. Market Cross	N. St. Anne's Church
C. Bath House	I. Old Hall Hotel	O. Victorian post box
D. St. Anne's Well	J. Opera House	P. Old Court House
E. Cavendish Arcade	K. Conservatory	Q. Old Devonshire Hospital,
F. Museum & Art Gallery	L. The Pavilion	now University of Derby campus

The Railway

The Midland Railway from Derby came to Buxton in 1863 and the London and North Western Railway from Manchester one year later, both running side by side into very similar style stations. Both of these stations had magnificent arched windows designed by Sir Joseph Paxton.

One of these windows, from the London and North West Railway station, can still be seen in situ.

Solomon's Temple

This folly, called Solomon's Temple, dominates the skyline at Buxton. It stands on the the summit of Grin Hill on the outskirts of Buxton. It was built in the 19th century by a man called Solomon Mycock, to give work to some of the unemployed in the town. It is built on the site of prehistoric graves, in which human skeletons were discovered.

The way to get to the landmark is to walk up along Broad Walk and follow the signs, past Poole's Cavern through Grindlow Woods.

As trains arrived carrying more and more tourists, patients and visitors eager to sample the town's charms and healing waters, more hotels and guest houses were built In order to help house them.

One of the largest was the Palace Hotel, built 1868 in the grand spa tradition, which stands close by the railway station. Another, The Grove Hotel, still retains the attractive stained glass entrance arch and canopies.

PICTURE: Courtesy of / copyright of Alan Walker of Poole's Cavern

The LNWR station window

Poole's Cavern

PICTURE: Courtesy of / copyright of Alan Walker of Poole's Cavern

Poole's Cavern on the southwestern outskirts of the town, is a large natural cave once used by the Romans and pre-historic man. It is a popular tourist attraction and has many fascinating formations.

The Souvenir Guide describes it as 'the fantastical results of a centuries old relationship between water and limestone. Like an inspired meeting between Salvador Dali and Fred Flintstone.'

The cavern was attracting visitors as early as the 16th century. Mary Queen of Scots is said to have visited in 1580 and Charles Cotton wrote about the cavern when he listed it as one of his 'Wonders of the Peak' in 1683.

Another famous visitor, the author Daniel Defoe, described the cavern in his book A Tour Through England and Wales, in 1724:

"South west from hence, about a quarter of a mile.... is a great cave or hole in the earth called Poole's Hole, ...It is a great cave, or natural vault, ancient doubtless as the mountain itself....It may be deepen'd and enlarged by streams an eruptions of subterraneous waters, of which here are several, as there generally are in such cavities....

Poole's Cavern became a show cave in 1853, when the first official custodian, Frank Redfern, was appointed. He enlarged the entrance and levelled the pathways.

Whilst digging he unearthed animal and human bones, some Roman coins, some broken Roman pottery and a bronze Roman brooch inlaid with silver. Other Roman jewellery found included brooches in the forms of a dolphin. a seahorse and a chariot wheel. Blobs of molten bronze and objects used for casting were also found, indicating a bronzesmith may have been based at the cavern.

There were also items found from even earlier people, with flints, bones and stone from the Late Neolithic (around 2,000 BC) and early Bronze Age (around 1,500BC) discovered.

Redfern also installed stairs and handrails to make access even easier. There was a museum and a bandstand then too. The museum was turned into a monkey house for a time as another attraction to the site.

When the show cave opened, lighting was in the form of huge candleabras. These were replaced in 1859 by the state

Some of the Roman jewellery found

of the art lighting of the day - 17 gas lights.

In 1965 the cavern closed, but in 1976 it was reopened with electric lights and new owners. The museum building was demolished in 1975, and many of the finds on display there went to Buxton Museum and Art Gallery. Today there is an award winning exhibition and visitor centre.

There were once tea parties held in the cavern and today there are still many special events held there, including candlelight tours, theatre and music.

Guided tours of Poole's Cavern last approximately 45 minutes and leave every 20 minutes throughout the day. There is a constant temperature of 7 degrees in the cavern so it is the same temperature whatever the weather above. There is a shop, play area and cafe, toilets and car parking.

■ Poole's Cavern,
Green Lane, Buxton, Derbyshire SK17 9DH
■ Telephone: 01298 26978
■ Email: info@poolescavern.co.uk
■ www.poolescavern.co.uk

Who was Poole?

An outlaw by the name of Poole. or Pole, lived in the cavern around 1400-1460 and it is thought this is where the name began. Families with the name Pole and Poole lived in Hartington and also the Wirral at the time.

One of the members of the Wirral family was outlawed for kidnapping, so it could perhaps be he who dodged justice and lived in the cavern.

"The story of one Pole or Poole, a famous giant or robber, (they might have well have called him a man eater) who harboured in this vault, and whose kitchen and lodging, or bedchamber, they show you on your right-hand, after you have crept about ten yards on all-four...."

Daniel Defoe, in his A Tour Through England and Wales, 1724, before the cavern was made easier to access by Redfern's efforts.

Grin Low Country Park

The view over Grin Low Country Park from Solomon's Temple

PICTURE: Courtesy of / copyright of Alan Walker of Poole's Cavern

There are many interesting formations in the cavern, caused by the action of rainwater on limestone. Amongst them are stalactities (pointing down) and stalagmites (pointing up). These 'icicles' found in caverns are made when the soft rock limestone dissolves in rainwater. Rainwater is a very dilute form of carbonic acid as it has absorbed carbon dioxide from the air. This water containing the dissolved limestone (calcium carbonate) seeps into the caverns. Tiny particles of the limestone then accumulate as water falls to the floor. Over the centuries the particles build up and get longer. These features have annual growth layers, similar to tree rings and are a good way of studying climate change. A wet year would have meant more growth on the stalactities and stalagmites. Here are just a few of the things you can see in the cavern:

■ POACHED EGG STALAGMITES: These are the most unusual and unique formations in Poole's Cavern. Their orange/red centre with white surround is what earns them the name, as it looks like the yolk of an egg.

The industry of 18th Century Lime burning on Grin Low created thousands of tons of fine waste lime powder, which was tipped above the cavern. The 'poached egg' stalagmites formed relatively quickly in such a unique colour and way in Poole's Cavern because of all this concentrated lime.

■ THE FLITCH OF BACON:

"And this forsooth the Bacon-Flitch they call,
Not that it does resemble one at all,
For it is round, not flat: but I suppose
Because it hangs i' th' roof, like one of those,
And shines like salt, Peak Bacon-eaters came
At first to call it by that greasy name.
CHARLES COTTON: THE WONDERS OF THE PEAK, 1681
This is a large stalactite that early visitors thought looked like half a pig, hung up in a butcher's shop. It is just under 2 metres (6.5 ft) long, but would be longer if it had not had its end broken off by vandals in the 19th century.

■ THE ORGAN CHAMBER:
Folded ribs of calcite in one part of the cavern look like the pipes of an organ. There is also a formation called the 'frozen waterfall.'

■ OTHER FEATURES: Also in the cavern is the Wedding Cake or Font, another very large stalagmite, and the great dome, rising to a height of 12 metres, as well as many other fascinating features.

Grin Low

Above the cavern is Grin Low Country Park. Now a scenic place to walk and enjoy the natural diversity, Grin Low was once full of lime kilns and the fumes from lime burning, as well as all the waste from the kilns. The quote below is from Adams' Gem of The Peak and describes the harsh conditions, with people even using the old lime kilns to live in:

"Almost the entire of Grin-low is covered with lime kilns. They gave this hill originally a strange and uncouth appearance, but the plantations now rapidly getting up, hide the greater part of them.
The hill is composed of a blueish limestone, admirably adapted for making lime of the very best quality, which is transported great distances.
In many of the old hillocks, composed of the dross and slag from the kiln and which are of great extent, some of the peasantry have formed themselves homes, called Lime Houses. `Breaking through the outer crust, which becomes exceedingly hard and waterproof, the parties excavate all the interior, wall it up inside and divide it make windows and perforate a hole through the top for the chimney, and by these means obtain a cheap and tolerable dwelling; but is said not to be healthy"

To try and reduce the eyesore, a 100 acre wood was planted by the 6th Duke of Devonshire around 1820.

Wood Anemone and Greater Spotted Woodpecker

The place is now a Site of Special Scientific Interest.and there are many species of wild plants, including field orchids to be found there.

Other plants you will probably see are Herb Robert, Herb Bennet, Wood anemone, Avens, Coltsfoot, Knapweed, Wild strawberry and Dog's mercury, It is also a good place for bird watching and you may be lucky enough to see a Tree-Creeper, Nuthatch, Greater Spotted Woodpecker, Woodcock, Redstart, Pied Fly-Catcher, Chiffchaff, Wood Warbler or Tawny Owl.

Chiffchaff

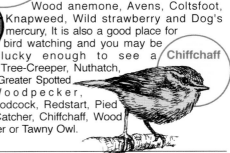

Lime burning

Top of a lime kiln at Millers Dale, with a wagon used to carry coal or limestone

One of the oldest industries in the Peak District is that of producing lime

PICTURE: Dave Sainty

L ime, produced from limestone, is a long used and very versatile product. It can be used for plastering, preparing animal hides, bleaching paper, whitewash and for agriculture. Since the White Peak is a limestone landscape, it's not surprising it has formed a major industry, both past and present, in this area.

A long known product

Limestone has not only provided many with stone for building houses and walls, it has also been used for limeburning,

The end product, lime or quicklime, has many applications; it was used in plaster work by the Egyptians about four thousand years ago. The Romans used lime to make a form of concrete.

For a big building project, a castle for instance, a lime kiln would be built on site, so builders could have immediate access to the material as needed for the lime mortar. These were usually temporary structures.

From the 17th century it was also used as a flux by smelters of lead and iron.

The effect of lime in contact with moisture also made it useful to sprinkle on cess pits - its caustic action killed off germs and helped decomposition

For hundreds of years 'slaked' lime has also been very important in agriculture, where it is used to reduce soil acidity in the soil and 'sweeten' it. Farmers often had their own lime burning kilns, with the kilns set in circular earthen mounds. There were many of these small farmers kilns, called pie, pudding pie, or pye kilns, in Derbyshire and the Peak District. The name probably derives from the round shape, like that of a pie. They were fired with timber, peat or furze.

One of the largest and earliest centres for limeburning in the Peak District was at Grin Low, south west of Buxton. In the 18th century there was a large limeburning complex there,

Another site was at Dove Holes. In the late 18th century Dove Holes was linked to the canal network by the Peak Forest Tramway and in the early 19th century the kilns at Grin Low were linked to the Cromford and High Peak Railway. This transport made the movement of lime products much easier and also the movement of the fuel for burning, coal, easier too.

Better transport meant that limeburning could be spread out further afield to places such as Millers Dale. and Cauldon Low. The building of more canal locks, bridges, docks etc for transport again helped to increase the need for lime mortar and so again increase the need for more kilns.

The kilns were often built in blocks, at harbours, near canals, or railway lines, to make better use of the transport links.

Kiln dotted

Some of the well known places in the Peak District were once very different, with the dirt of industry making them places to avoid, not the tourist attractions we know today. They were dotted with lime kilns and tainted with the associated pollution.

The pretty village of Stoney Middleton, now a popular place famed for its well dressing, had a reputation in the late 18th century, as an unhealthy place. There were many lime kilns there and the area was under a constant pall of acrid smoke.

It was a busy spot with constant to-ings and fro-ings to feed and empty the kilns. Cart-loads of coal were brought in from Sheffield and Chesterfield, returning with processed lime.

In the 1851 guide book to the area, Gem of The Peak, the author, Adam, describes the place:

"The Dale is narrow...to the left is banded by a lofty range and dotted almost the entire way by lime kilns.

"A powerful stream runs through the Dale, generally discoloured by the refuse from the kilns, which destroys its beauty".

Mass production

The continued increase in need meant that kilns became designed to be in constant use, and so more permanent and well made. By the 20th century it was a mass production and kilns were often near, or at, a larger quarry.

Brick kilns were built when there was enough stone to do so and these could be re-used. The lime kilns surviving today are usually the sturdier 18th and 19th century ones.

Lime kilns and the process of lime burning

Chemistry

Lime is derived from chalk or limestone, which is calcium carbonate - $CaCO_3$. Limestone rock is formed from the shells and skeletons of sea creatures that die and sink to the sea bed.

When calcium carbonate ($CaCO_3$) is heated (to around 1000 degrees C), it drives out the gas carbon dioxide (CO_2).

This leaves calcium oxide (CaO), also known as quicklime.

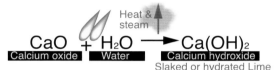

$$CaCO_3 \longrightarrow CaO$$

Limestone — Calcium oxide
Quick Lime

Carbon dioxide given off
CO_2
$1000^\circ C$

When limestone is burnt, it will only produce half of the original quantity of quicklime, which is why so many kilns and so much burning was needed to keep up with demand.

If put with water, (H_2O) quicklime reacts violently and produces heat, enough to create steam. The result is calcium hydroxide ($Ca(OH)_2$, also known as slaked or hydrated lime.

$$CaO + H_2O \longrightarrow Ca(OH)_2$$

Calcium oxide — Water — Calcium hydroxide
Slaked or hydrated Lime
Heat & steam

Slaked lime, left in the open, slowly reacts with carbon dioxide and water in the atmosphere to once again become calcium carbonate.

Mortar

It is this fact of reverting back to calcium carbonate and going hard again, that means it is ideal material for holding things together, as in mortar. To make mortar, quicklime is mixed with sand, then water added to make a stiff paste.

As reversion back to calcium carbonate takes place, (slowly enough to do things with first, such as build walls etc), the mortar gets hard. It can continue hardening and getting stronger for years. If silica and alumina are put in to the mixture, it gets even harder, and also hardens under water, ideal for bridges etc. This type of cement is called hydraulic.

Limewash

Slaked lime was used as a whitewash on the walls of buildings. This coating has a greater permeability than other paints, so buildings can 'breathe' better.

The method is again popular as a more 'green' paint, especially when restoring old buildings. Colour can be added to the wash and can be seen on many gold and pink shaded cottages such as in the Cotswolds and Suffolk.

Types of kiln

Periodic kiln: as the name suggests, not always in use, but was emptied and then reloaded in between.

Draw kiln: used continuously, with raw material and fuel added in at the top as it is used up and the burnt quicklime drawn off at the bottom. It is usually draw type kilns which still survive now.

Flare kiln: when the fuel is kept separate from the limestone, which means that the resulting burnt lime is free from ash.

Mixed feed kiln: the limestone and fuel are mixed together. .

Domed tops or chimneys were sometimes built over the top of the limekilns. As well as making it safer (without these there was nothing to stop people falling into the top of a kiln and onto the burning contents), the chimneys made controlling draughts easier and protected the contents from bad weather. Also if demand was low the kiln chimney could be shut off to keep it hot until more was needed and so more limestone etc put in.
The chimneys had to have doors in them to put in the raw materials.

A typical draw kiln would be lined with stone or fire bricks, and usually shaped like an inverted cone. The kiln would be loaded with alternating layers of limestone and coal. Iron bars at the bottom supported it all. Under the bars was set the fire, with wood as fuel.

As the burnt lime fell to the bottom, the bars could be adjusted for drawing it off through the 'eye' or draw hole. Sometimes there is a poking or 'tool' hole above the draw hole, through which ash can be cleared and the lime can be poked about to make it settle to the bottom better. Sometimes there are little doors for the limeburner to look in and check the temperature and to see if it is all burning ok.

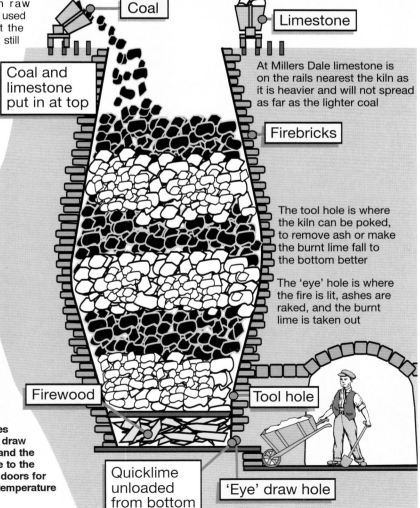

Coal

Limestone

Coal and limestone put in at top

At Millers Dale limestone is on the rails nearest the kiln as it is heavier and will not spread as far as the lighter coal

Firebricks

The tool hole is where the kiln can be poked, to remove ash or make the burnt lime fall to the bottom better

The 'eye' hole is where the fire is lit, ashes are raked, and the burnt lime is taken out

Firewood

Tool hole

Quicklime unloaded from bottom

'Eye' draw hole

Millers Dale

Kilns to the west of Millers Dale, with concrete supporting buttresses, added later

East kilns

Lime Kilns at Millers Dale

West kiln eye

East kiln 'eye' where lime was taken out

The village

The village of Miller's Dale once had water-powered corn mills, but later, after the opening of the new turnpike road between Tideswell and Buxton in 1812 which provided easier access, more mills moved to the area, producing timber, silk and cotton.

The amount of mills gave Miller's Dale its name.

Miller's Dale was once an important railway junction, where passengers for Buxton joined or left the trains between London and Manchester on the old Midland Railway. There was a large railway station which served local villages and industries alike.

Rail provided easier access to the limestone deposits. The quarries expanded and the village grew as housing was built for the rail men and quarry workers and their families.

Around 1880 a lime works opened up above the station, with lime-kilns built alongside the track. These were worked until 1944. During the second world war metal caps had to be fitted on the top of them, so enemy aircraft could not see the flames. Remains of these limekilns can still be seen.

On top of these kilns are two overlapping narrow gauge tracks These brought limestone from the nearby quarry and coal from the railway sidings below.

Limestone was tipped from the inner rails and coal from the outer. (Coal, being lighter spread further.) 100 tons of limestone and 20 tons of coal produced about 56 tons of quicklime.

At the bottom of the kilns, you can go into the tunnels where the quicklime was removed.

From Track to Trail

The railway is now closed, a casualty of the Beeching cuts, but Millers Dale is still dominated by huge railway viaducts. When the line closed, the remaining quarries closed too, and the lime works was demolished in 1971

The Peak National Park Authority took over the old line in 1980 and converted it into the extremely popular Monsal Trail. The old limestone quarries are now nature reserves. The area is a wonderful place to see wild flowers. There are cowslips, early purple orchid, harebell and wild strawberries among the flowers. Other parts of the reserve have valerian, rosebay willowherb and ladies bedstraw.

So many plants means lots of butterflies and insects. One butterfly you may spot is the Common Blue.

Harebells and a Common Blue

The cart on the rail tracks on top of the west kilns

PICTURES: Courtesy of / copyright of Dave Sainty

Many jobs were associated with lime burning. There were the burners, whose wages depended on the amount of lime they produced, and drawers, or pikers, who brought out the burnt lime from 'eyes' at the bottom of the kilns. After being removed, the burnt lime was sorted from the ash by pickers and taken to the railway wagons. Sometimes the limestone hadn't burnt properly and was still hard in the middle. As much lime as possible was knocked off the lump before the raw stone was discarded. The person doing this was called a 'bull head knocker.'

Looking at flowers in an old quarry in Miller's Dale

Florence Nightingale

When people think of the Crimean War, one of the names that first comes to mind is not of a soldier or a general, but a woman, Florence Nightingale. Florence did much to help and publicise the plight of the soldiers and later to revolutionise the hospital system.

The Nightingales

This family, from which the famous Florence was descended was a well to-do one, after making money through various industrial investments and projects. One member of the family Peter Nightingale, established a lead smelting business at Lea Bridge, near Cromford, and extended an arm of the Cromford Canal to serve it.

When Peter Nightingale died he left his estate and money to his nephew, William Edward Shore.

William changed his name to Nightingale when he inherited in 1820 and soon married a woman named Frances.

The couple were wealthy and travelled extensively. They had two daughters, Florence and Parthenope, who were both born abroad. Florence was born in Florence, Italy on 12th May, 1820. Her sister was born a year earlier in Naples. (Parthenope is the Greek name for Naples).

When they returned to England, in 1825, William built a grand house for his bride and family, Lea Hurst, in the village of Holloway. His wife, however, didn't like it so he also bought a home in Hampshire, Emberley House

After that they only used Lea Hurst in the summer months. William educated his daughters at home, with more varied and intellectual subjects perhaps than many women would have had at the time. Not surprisingly, the academic and intelligent Florence was not happy to stay at home and wait for a husband. She refused a proposal of marriage, knowing it was not right for her.

Florence informed her parents she wanted to be a nurse. They were against it, and thought it unfitting of her social status, even though Florence felt she had been called by God to follow this path. But Florence was determined and in 1851 trained in Kaiserwerth, near Dusseldorf, and Paris. and then worked in London, all the time gaining nursing knowledge and experience and developing her own ideas.

A chance to serve

In March 1854, the Crimean War began. Newspaper reports told of wounded soldiers and the terrible conditions they were enduring, with no proper facilities to treat them.

Many women wrote in offering service as volunteers and goverment minister Sidney Herbert, who knew of Florence's work and capabilities, asked her to co-ordinate these volunteers. Florence did so and took 38 nurses to Barrack Hospital in Scutari, a suburb of Constantinople.

At first the doctors there did not ask for their help, but the amount of casualties coming in made them give in and let the women aid them.

Dethick, Lea and Holloway are a historic cluster of villages each with a famous resident. The 'Lady of the Lamp' who lived at Holloway, is one of the most well known

Florence worked to improve standards and comfort at the hospital. She used to do tours of inspection at night, with a lamp, hence the nickname. She became an iconic figure written about in the newspapers, with songs and poems penned describing her noble work.

But Florence hated this romantised image of her, used as a symbol of saintly virtue and for sanitised propaganda. In August 1856, when she returned home to Holloway, at Whatstandwell Station, she carried her own bags back to Lea Hurst, turning her back on the limelight.

Florence Nightingale 1820 - 1910

A632

A6

A615

MATLOCK

Matlock Bath

A5012

Dethick

Lea

Holloway

Cromford

Whatstandwell

A6

Major achievements

Back home at Lea Hurst in the quiet village of Holloway, Florence did not rest for long, or lessen her determination to improve medical care and conditions in hospitals. In November 1856, she went to London to ask for Royal Commission to investigate conditions in the army hospitals.

When Florence looked at the statistics of deaths from disease in the army field hospital and at the Scutari hospital, she was distressed to find that more people had died at Scutari. This was due to insanitary conditions and water supply - the hospital was over a sewer and the water supply was contaminated.

These figures could maybe have made Florence feel she had failed in her duties to help improve things, but, still determined, she put her energy into further ventures. For all her work with statistics, she became the first woman to be elected a Fellow of the Statistical Society.

Florence also founded nurse training schools, the first of which was St Thomas' in London. She also wrote extensively on hospital planning and organisation. In 1860, she wrote her best known work, Notes on Nursing. In recognition of her tireless work, Queen Victoria awarded Florence the Royal Red Cross in 1883.

Poor health

Later in life Florence Nightingale was not a well women and became bedridden. Maybe her illness was to do with the harsh conditions in the Crimea, but it could have started earlier than that, in childhood.

In Florence's 'Curriculum Vitae' she writes that she had a sickly childhood *"I never learned to write till I was 11 or 12, owing to a weakness in my hands."* Other members of the family had poor health too- *"My sister has always had delicate health"... "My nephew ...was a sickly child."*

The proximity of lead works to the village of Holloway could have been a factor in this ill health. Lead poisoning in children causes 'drop wrist' which is a weakness in the wrists. A child with lead poisoning can be difficult and can also become reclusive. Florence didn't like eating with guests, and was shy and sometimes reclusive.

As well as the lead, the nearby hat factory would have been a possible source of mercury, which was used in the hat making process. Mercury effects the kidneys, brain and nervous system, sometimes causing mental health problems. People who made hats often suffered these problems, hence the 'Mad Hatter' in Alice in Wonderland and the saying 'as mad as a hatter.'

A pet owl

Florence had a pet owl which she rescued from teasing boys beneath the walls of the Acropolis in Italy in 1850. The owl, a baby Little Owl (Athene Noctua) had fallen from her nest. The sisters called the owl Athena. The owl was brought back to England and was a companion for Florence until she died around the time Florence was leaving for the Crimea. One story is that she was trapped in the attic in the bustle of Florence leaving, and died. Another is that the owl died of a broken heart because her mistress left. Parthenope wrote a biography and described how Athena used to sit on Florence's head or be carried around in her pocket.

Florence was so heartbroken at the owl's death that she had her embalmed. And Athena still survives, stuffed, sitting on a branch in a glass case. She was at Lea Hurst for many years and stayed there when the house became a residential home. When Lea Hurst was sold again in 2006, Athena's new home became Florence Nightingale Museum in St. Thomas' Hospital, London.

This museum has many of Florence's possessions, including a medicine chest, dress, Scutari Hospital sash, and writings. There is also a lamp thought to be the same as the famous lady used, a Turkish lantern from Scutari Hospital during the Crimean War. Unlike the popular idea depicted in images of Florence, it is not glass but of a concertina design, made of waxy paper.

■ Florence Nightingale Museum, St Thomas' Hospital, 2 Lambeth Palace Road, London SE1 7EW
■ Tel: 020 7620 0374
■ www.florence-nightingale.co.uk
■ email: info@florence-nightingale.co.uk

Florence's lamp probably looked like this

Nightingale Chapel, Holloway

This converted Primitive Methodist chapel, dated 1852, has Florence Nightingale's name on the original deeds.

It is close to the centre of Holloway, on Chapel Lane and is now a holiday cottage. www.florencenightingalechapel.co.uk

Florence's old home, Lea Hurst, is now a private home so please respect this if you visit Holloway.

Lea

Athena the owl

The lead and hat factories near Lea Bridge, close to Holloway, and the mill that now houses Smedley's, used the green power of the waters as the quote below describes:

"Nothing cam be more pleasant and beautiful than the situation of the hamlet - the limpid mountain stream playing through it, pressed into the service of the various manufacturies."
From Gem of The Peak by W. Adam (1851)

At the village can be found Lea Gardens, where, in April, May and June there is a lovely display of rhododendrons and azaleas, alpines and conifers. There is also a tea shop with gifts for sale.
■ Tel: 01629 534380.

Sheffield Connections

Florence Nightingale also had connections with the city of Sheffield. Tapton Hall, on Shore Lane at Fulwood, is on the site of the earlier Tapton House, which in the eighteenth century it was the home of members of the Shore Family.

Mary Shore, who lived there, was great Aunt to Florence Nightingale. (Her father was originally called William Shore as mentioned earlier). Florence used to visit her aunt at the house

In 1855 the steel magnate Edward Vickers built Tapton Hall. In 1867 this hall became home to George Wilson, of Wilson's Snuff at Sharrow, near Hunter's Bar.

By 1965 the Sheffield Masonic Hall Company had taken over the hall. It was extended in 1967.

There is a monument to members of the Shore family of Tapton Hall at Ecclesall Church, Sheffield, on an interior wall.

Dethick

Not far from Holloway and Lea is another place with historic connections, Dethick. This tiny hamlet of three farms and a church was once home to a man behind a plot to kill Queen Elizabeth the First- Anthony Babington.

During the 13th century a manor house and adjoining chapel was built by Geoffrey Dethick. A daughter of the family married into the Babington family and by the 15th century the Babington family had inherited the manor and chapel. The chapel is dedicated to St. John the Baptist.

Anthony Babington (October 24, 1561 – September 20, 1586) , was born into this wealthy Catholic family As a child Babington had served as a page to Mary while she was imprisoned at Sheffield. It is likely that it was during this time Babington became a supporter of Mary's cause to ascend to the throne.

He and other conspirators were young English Catholic noblemen, who wanted to remove Elizabeth, a Protestant, and replace her with Mary, a fellow Catholic.

The Babington Plot

Sir Francis Walsingham, Elizabeth's Principal Secretary, found out about letters which told of the plans, but allowed them to continue to be sent because he wanted to discover who else was involved in this plot and try and implicate Mary.

However, Mary had written her correspondence with the conspirators in a 'substitution cipher'. This is where one letter of the alphabet is swopped for another from a list held by both writer and recipient. Here is a very simple example:

Alphabet: A B C D E F G H I J K L M N O P Q R S T
Substitute: T S R Q P O N M L K J I H G F E D C B A

If writing an A you would use the substituted letter T instead.
So OPEN THE DOOR would be FEPG AMP QFFC.

The same code was known to the others in the plot, who would have the same list of substituted letters and so could translate the code back into the original message.

But the code Mary and her plotters used was quickly deciphered by Walsingham and his helpers, and translations were provided for Elizabeth. The letters were then resealed and sent on to their destination or delivered to Mary in prison.

Eventually, in 1586, Mary wrote a letter to Babington. In his reply, Babington told Mary that he and a group of six friends were planning to murder Elizabeth.

This was the evidence Walsingham needed. When the letter from Mary asking for details was intercepted, a postscript was forged in her hand asking for the identities of the plotters.

This was done and the letter with their names was duly intercepted too, giving the evidence needed for their arrest.

Treason

The plotters were duly arrested and convicted of plotting the assassination of Elizabeth I of England and conspiring with Mary. What became known as the "Babington Plot" and Mary's alleged involvement in it led her to be charged with treason, which led to her execution. Babington and six others were also executed, for high treason, on 18 September, 1586. Their punishment was to be hung, drawn and quartered.

On 20th September, the men were tied face downwards on a hurdle drawn by horses and dragged through the streets of London. At Tyburn they were hung for a short period. After being revived they then had their intestines drawn out whilst still alive.

After this the executioner chopped and quartered their bodies and distributed the parts to prominent locations around the city to warn others against trying the same crime.

Queen Elizabeth is reputed to have been so disturbed by reports of the horrific executions she ordered that the remaining conspirators should be left to hang until dead before being disembowelled.

Mary denied all knowledge of the plot, but the letters were produced as evidence of her guilt. After months of delays Elizabeth signed Mary's death warrant on 1 February 1587. Seven days later she was beheaded at Fotheringay Castle.

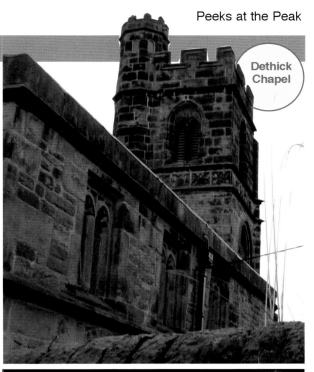

Dethick Chapel

The simple and beautiful interior of the Chapel

The key for the chapel can be collected from the old dairy of the nearby Manor House

There are lovely views from outside the chapel

Lathkill Dale

The River Lathkill is one of Derbyshire's smaller rivers, but it makes up with beauty and a very impressive valley

The River Lathkill, one of the purest in the country

This beautiful valley is a splendid place to appreciate nature, but also to appreciate the industrial heritage of the area, now mellowed to give a special character.

Lathkill Dale is situated 2 miles south west of Bakewell, between the villages of Over Haddon, Monyash and Youlgrave. It is one of the dales which makes up the Derbyshire Dales National Nature Reserve.

Monyash

This village is one of the places from which to access Lathkill Dale. Monyash (or `Many-ash`) was so named because of the amount of ash trees once there.

Mining brought prosperity to the village during the 18th and 19th centuries. There is a public house called the Bull's Head on the village green. It is one of the oldest buildings in the village, dating from the late 17th/ early 18th century and used to host Derbyshire's 'Barmote' (a court which dealt with lead mining disputes and other activities and was also responsible for lead mining administration). There is an Ashford Marble floor just inside the entrance.

Monyash church has been extensively restored, but dates originally from the late 12th century. There is also a Methodist Chapel constructed in 1888.

One Ash Grange, farmed by the monks of Roche Abbey during the Middle Ages. It is about half a mile away on the eastern edge of the village

Hay meadows are being recreated around the Monyash entrance to Lathkill Dale to improve the area and wildlife.

Over Haddon

Over Haddon is the other place to access Lathkill Dale. It is an interesting village, with a church, St Anne's, that is the resting place of a former head of MI6, Maurice Oldfield.

The disapprearing river

Lathkill Dale is not entirely natural, having been shaped in places by man's hand, for it was once a busy lead mining spot. There are still shafts and drainage channels but they are now blending into the landscape and add interest.

One consequence of the mines was that the water table was lowered, and each summer the river dries out in parts. It stays dry for about a kilometre until it reaches Lathkill Head Cave, where the water re-emerges.

As the water gets lower, stranded fish need to be rescued and The Environment Agency lends a hand. To do this they use a technique known as 'electric fishing'.

Electrodes are first placed in the water. Fish are attracted by the electrical current which is picked up by the 'lateral line' - a sensor on their bodies.

As the fish get closer, they are mildly stunned and so can be collected into baskets, moved into a tank and then moved to the deeper part of the river. It is mainly brown trout (pictured) that are found in the parts of the river that dry up. In deeper parts with constant flow there are bull head and brook lamprey.

A dipper- often to be seen at Lathkill Dale

A fascinating valley

Limestone

The landscape around Lathkill Dale is good example of KARST landscape. This is a landscape that is formed when the rock below is dissolved by the weak acid created when carbon dioxide dissolves in water. This means there are lots of caves and good drainage.

Fossils of the sea creatures from which limestone is formed can be spotted around the area, in rocks or in walls.

Crinoids, or sea lilies are one form of fossil you may see. They are animals not plants and were once attached to the sea bed. They were protected by a layer of calcium carbonate which is the part which is now preserved as fossils. Crinoids are also known also known as 'Derbyshire Screws' as the parts of the stems in the rock look a bit like screws.

Fossil remains of crinoids, or sea lillies

Tufa

Tufa is light brown, full of holes, and looks a bit like pumice.

It is formed when calcium carbonate in water deposits on plants, algae etc and gradually solidifies. This can be seen at Lathkill Dale.

Corn mills

Farmers including the monks had corn mills in the area. There used to be three but only traces of one remains, the ruins of Carters Mill, including the mill pond and weirs.

A Moorhen and right, a Grey Wagtail

This is a good spot to see Grey Wagtails, Moorhens and Coots.

The other mills were Over Haddon Mill, which was where Lathkill Lodge is now and Conksbury mill, gone without trace and last recorded in 1617.

Farming

One of the earliest signs of man living and using the dale which still survives is an early medieval sheep-wash. The remains are still there and it was till used to wash sheep before shearing until as late as 1940s.

A foolish gold rush

This began in 1854 with rumours that gold had been found in one of the lead mines at Lathkill Dale. Over Haddon was full of would be gold-diggers, many people invested and lost money as the amount of gold was was so deep and in such small quantities it was totally unviable.

Conksbury Bridge

Conksbury Bridge. This medieval bridge carries the Youlgreave to Bakewell road across the river. The river goes on towards Alport and later joins with the River Wye near Haddon Hall.

The bridge was reputedly built by the monks to get supplies to and from Bakewell.

Ricklow Quarry

During the 18th and 19th centuries the area was well known for grey marble, a form of limestone, which was extracted from this quarry. There are lots of fossils in the stone here, but if you go to look take care as it is a difficult path and can be dangerous.

Flora

A good time to visit Lathkill Dale is in May or June, as the wildflowers are most abundant then.

Lots of wildflowers can grow as there are not many nutrients and the soil is only shallow and drains easily. No large plants, which need more food and water, can compete. Jacob's Ladder, a rare plant which flowers in June and July, is found in Lathkill Dale, as is Yellow Archangel, Early Purple Orchids and Cowslips. Other limestone indicator plants such as Common Rock Rose, Hart's Tongue and salad burnet are abundant.

The area is a Site of Special Scientific Interest and also a conservation area. Please take care not to damage the flowers and please don't pick any.

So many flowers mean Lathkill is also a good place to spot butterflies, such as the Brown Argus, or moths, such as the day flying Cistus Forester, whose metallic green wings you may see flitting around the Rock Rose.

Yellow Archangel and (below) Jacob's Ladder, left, & Cowslip

Early Purple Orchid

Rock Rose and Cistus Forester moth

Monyash

Toilets

Ricklow Quarry

A good place to see the rare plant Jacobs Ladder

Lathkill Head Cave - source of the River Lathkill

Remains of Medieval sheep wash

Waterfall- a good spot to see dippers

Carters Mill millpond

Bateman's House

Toilets

P Over Haddon

Mandale Engine House

Aquaduct

Mandale Mine and Engine House

Lathkill Dale has long been a place where lead mining was carried out. In Roman times the Peak was already well known for lead production.

The Mandale Mine at Lathkill Dale was one of the earliest recorded in Derbyshire, being worked from the 13th century. The richest lead ore was below the water table and extracting it was dangerous due to the mines flooding.

A huge waterwheel was built to power pumps to remove water from the mine shaft. The pillars that supported the aqueduct which served this waterwheel can still be seen.

In the 1840`s there was an attempt to drain the deep mines by building a steam engine. The engine that pumped was the type called a Beam Engine and the engine house still remains as an evocative ruin.

The beam engine would have been at the top of what is now the tallest remaining wall of the engine house.

One end of the beam was attached to a steam engine. The other end was attached to rods that worked pumps underground to push water from the mine shafts.

Pressure from the steam engine pushed the beam engine pistons up and down, making the beam engine move in a rocking motion. As the end attached to the steam engine went up, the end attached to the rods went down and collected water. Then the steam was released, the end attached to the steam engine went down and the end attached to the rods came up, and lifted and pushed the water up and away from the mineshaft down drainage channels.

Even with this engine, the best technology of the day, flooding was still a problem and the mine was closed by the 1850s.

Beam engine

This end was attached to the steam engine

How the beam engine may have looked when in place

This end attached to rods going down to pump

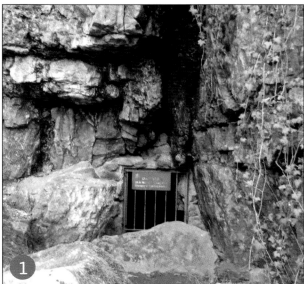

1. Mandale Mine entrance 2. Steps up to engine house from footpath 3. Remains of aqueduct 4. Engine House

Bateman's House

Who was Bateman?

These ruins of a house at Lathkill Dale were once home to a man called James Bateman. He was an agent working for The Lathkill Mine Company in the 1830s. This company had been set up in 1825 by two men named Thomas Bateman and John Alsop, to try and mine the deeper lead there.

What became a house may have been an industrial building to start with, with doors windows and fireplaces perhaps added later.

Hidden secret

Steps down to the mine shaft top

The building is an usual place for a home, because it is built over a deep leadmine shaft. According to the information boards at the site, records suggest that James Bateman installed a large pump in the shaft.

Tools of the miner - a pick and a 'bucking iron' used for breaking up large lumps of ore

The pump was a new type called a disc pump' and the building over it could originally have been built to house mechanism for hoisting the heavy pump into place, or perhaps it was to hide it from people who may have seen it and stolen the idea.

House keeping

There has been a lot of work by Natural England and English Heritage to repair the house and made it visitable. Lots of work clearing rubble, replacing beams and repairing walls have improved the site immensely. There is a a ladder down to see the top of the shaft underneath the house, where the pump would have been. Lights have also been installed, powered by a hand driven generator in the mine shaft.

Lathkill Dale is one of five dales in the White Peak that make up the Derbyshire Dales National Nature Reserve. Natural England takes care of these dales.
■ Natural England, 'Endcliffe' Deepdale Business Park, Ashford Road, Bakewell, Derbyshire DE45 1GT
■ Tel: 01629 816640 ■ Email: peak.derbys@naturalengland.org.uk ■ www.naturalengland.org.uk

---

The ruins of Bateman's House

Natural beauty

Lambs play at Lathkill Dale in the spring sunshine

Some views of Lathkill Dale

Peach of a theatre

The Playhouse at Great Hucklow in 1965

Great Hucklow, in the Peak District, once laid claim to being the smallest village in England with its own professional theatre

PICTURE: Courtesy of Sheffield Newspapers

Anyone who read one of the earlier Ladybird children's books may have sampled the work of the man behind the formation of the theatre at Great Hucklow, Lawrence du Garde Peach.

Literary merit

Lawrence du Garde Peach (1890-1974) was a former writer for Punch magazine and also for a lot of the Ladybird children's book series, as well as Children's Hour.

He was born in Conduit Road, Sheffield, the son of a Unitarian minister and his wife.

Peach was educated at Manchester Grammar School and soon it was evident he had acting ability. He carried on his education at Manchester University, studying English Language and English Literature .

In the First World War he was involved in Military intelligence and reached the rank of captain. He also married during the war, in September 1915.

After the war Peach took a PhD at Sheffield University, later becoming employed as a lecturer in Exeter.

Whilst in Exeter he also worked as a freelance journalist. He worked for various publications, including Punch and gave up his lecturing job to concentrate on writing.

He also spread out into radio drama and playwriting, He did many history/biography type productions for Children's Hour on the radio as well as composing film scripts.

Great Hucklow theatre

In 1918 Peach's father changed jobs, taking up a post as the official minister at Great Hucklow. Soon afterwards Lawrence and his wife also moved to the Peak District village..

It was here, in Great Hucklow, that Lawrence founded the Village Players, who performed some of the plays Peach had written, as well Shakespeare ones and many others. The actors and staff were mostly from the local area.

The theatre became very popular and productions were frequently sold out.

Peach also made a few some short films, including Derbyshire Under Snow (1933).

He also had close connections with the Sheffield Repertory Company at Sheffield Playhouse.

Peach never wrote a biography, but his book 'Twenty Five Years of Play Producing 1927 - 1952, is a great insight.

He died at his home in Foolow on the 31at December 1974, two years after his wife.

The Sheffield Playhouse in 1975

PICTURE: Courtesy of Sheffield Newspapers

The Great Hucklow Village Players

A written record

Lawrence du Garde Peach wrote a book about The Village Players, called "Twenty Five Years of Play Producing 1927 - 1952".

It is a fascinating and amusing book, and gives an insight into the passion, commitment and hard work that went into the group over the decades.

In his foreword, Peach describes their theatre as a

"well equipped and acoustically perfect theatre, with an excellent stage, twenty eight feet wide from wall to wall and with more than thirty feet of depth. It has first class lighting, a cyclorama, a practical grid and a steeply raked auditorium seating 266 people; it contains the usual Green Room, dressing rooms, workshop, scene dock etc., and outside it are two car parks, with accommodation for a hundred cars."

Not the usual scale of production for a small village.

Peach's book tells of how this theatre company in a remote Derbyshire village had a far flung reputation and drew people from all over the country. The plays were famed for never stinting on effects and quality. Peach cast and produced every play. Actors were only chosen for parts if they were suitable; if the right person could not be found for a part, the play was dropped. There were no membership subscriptions in the company and people gained a part by merit alone.

The photographs in the book serve to show how good a quality the productions were in terms of sets and costume. They have the classic elegance of movie stills.

A page from Peach's book showing the later home of the players, the Playhouse

THE VILLAGE PLAYERS
GREAT HUCKLOW

present

TWENTY-FIVE YEARS OF PLAY PRODUCING
1927—1952

A RECORD

compiled by
L. du Garde Peach

THE PLAYHOUSE
The lower car park

THE PLAYHOUSE

The beginning

Around 1887, Peach's father, in his role as Unitarian Minister in Sheffield, began taking children out into the Peak District from his Sunday School. They went to Great Hucklow for a week's holiday in the summer.

Many children, from other Sunday schools, began staying in the village for part of the summer too, and a special building was erected as a holiday home,

By 1918 Peach's father moved to Great Hucklow, soon after followed by his son Lawrence, who was already familiar with the place and its people, having spent a lot of his time there over the years.

During the winter months, the holiday home was empty and in 1927 Lawrence decided to use it as a theatre.

The Merchant of Venice was chosen as the first production and he recruited his whole cast at The Old Chapel Party, an annual event for villagers held in the holiday home.

Production

Before they could perform, a stage had to be built. Also there was the problem of lighting as the village had no electricity. This was solved with a few accumulators from a battery company in Bakewell, which were used to power a dozen car headlight bulbs. Peach says in his book:

"It was simple to use and easy to dim. Occasionally it even dimmed itself."

This set up was used until 1932, when electricity was brought to the village.

Peach played the part of Shylock and had to learn lines as well as help sort all the other things out, such as publicity, (a Tideswell printer did the posters etc.), selling tickets, box

office staff and more. Costumes were begged from the wardrobes and sewing rooms of the villagers. The Doge of Venice in the play was dressed in old crimson curtains from a four poster bed. Only the tights were bought. Sets were simple and effective, built in a barn and conveyed to the holiday home theatre by milk float.

The playbill advertised the play as going on 'at the time of the full moon' which may sound oddly old fashioned but was very practical when there were no street lamps to help the audience make their way there.

The dates were March 17th, 18th and 19th 1927 and tickets cost one and twopence for adults (about 5.5 pence), and sixpence (2.5 pence) for children. The play wasn't a sell out and people seemed bemused by it all, but the players were eager to have another go when the summer was over and the home was free again.

But perhaps eager is too active a word. According to Peach:

"Even if the audience were not clamouring for it, the players were. Well, perhaps clamouring is not quite the word. We do not clamour in Derbyshire. Put it rather that from time to time members of the cast hinted off-handedly that maybe if sometime we had another shot at a play it wouldn't be amiss. That, in Derbyshire, represents a very considerable degree of enthusiasm."

The Village Players
GREAT HUCKLOW
will present

THE
MERCHANT
OF
VENICE
by
William Shakespeare
in the
HOLIDAY HOME
GREAT HUCKLOW
at the time of the Full Moon
Thursday, March 17th
Friday, March 18th
Saturday, March 19th
at 8 O'CLOCK.
Admission 1s 2d.   Children 6d.   By Ticket

On with the shows

It was in December of the same year that the 'another shot at a play' happened, when the group did a week's run of Twelfth Night. There had been no preparations inbetween and no idea that there would be a development into a long running theatre group.

The programme for Twelfth Night carried an image that was to become the group's trade mark- a rectangle containing a crouching figure.

Having fun

Peach and the others were having fun and the holiday home was not needed until March, so he decided to do another production after Christmas, not Shakespeare this time, but Shaw's Arms and the Man, for a run of three nights.

A 1952 programme showing the trademark crouching figure

After that it was back to Shakespeare with As You Like It, with the next production being Pygmalion, followed by a double bill of Everyman and The Shepherd's Play.

By the time of this production, the audience had built up nicely, though were still local. Ticket sales were still not covering the cost of the plays, but their confidence was growing. The holiday home was now publicised as 'The Playhouse.'

A new home

The Village Players became quite an institution and needed a more solid and permanent home. In March 1938, after a production of The Silver King, the holiday home was no longer used as a theatre. Instead they took over an stone old building, a cupola, once used for smelting lead, at the opposite end of the village from the holiday home.

A lot of work as needed to turn the dirty old building into a theatre.Some of the seats were a bargain buy from the Montgomery Hall in Sheffield, which had just had a refit.

The first audience came in October 1938, with an eclipse during the opening week - an apt sign for the players who performed at the full moon and kept the fact written on their playbills until the play runs became too long to fit within the full moon's phase.

The opening was a multiple bill of four one act plays written by Peach, 'Business is Business', 'The Doomed Village', 'Mrs Grundy Comes to Tea' and 'Shells'.

When war broke out in 1939 many of players were in the home guard, joined the forces or were working in the Civil Defence Organisation.

Matinee performances were given, with more shows in summer, to avoid the problems of blackout and many people arrived by bicycle due to petrol shortages.

The performances continued, though not as often and usually with an upbeat theme to cheer people up. One performance in 1941 was of Peach's Home Guard comedy, 'According to Plan'. No problem with costumes or realism of course, as most of the cast were in the Home Guard anyhow. Peach says that the George Formy Home Guard film was based on it, though was not impressed by the result.

End of an era

After the war the plays continued, including special performances for Youth Groups, which seemed to be almost too popular:

"It was a revelation. We had no idea that youth lasted so long in Derbyshire. Most of them had to be helped up and down the steps. It was our last special performance for Youth Groups."

The players also broadcast some one act plays on the BBC, or broadcast as individuals. Some plays were recorded at the Playhouse itself.

In 1949 the Players celebrated their twenty first birthday (a year late) at The Maynard Arms Hotel in Grindleford.

As Peach wrote his record of Twenty Five Years the Players were performing a thriller called The Late Edwina Black. Peach closes his story of the company with these words:

"This account will, in the years to come, be all that remains to witness to the fact that once a theatre existed and throve in this little Peakland village, that once far - travelled cars parked about this old cupola barn, transformed by the magic of words and lights and cunningly contrived effects, into the exciting world of the theatre."

The grand little theatre closed in 1972. The magic was stilled and the last curtain closed. The building is still there and at time of writing is used as an outdoor pursuit centre.

Ladybird Books

In the 1950s Lawrence di Garde Peach was commissioned to write for the Ladybird series of children's books, over 20 titles in all. They were on historical and biographical themes and were very popular.

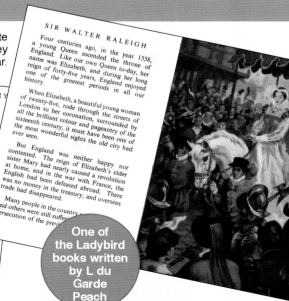

One of the Ladybird books written by L du Garde Peach

Bolsover Castle

The frontage of the Little Castle at Bolsover

This 17th century jewel was built as a pleasure palace for entertaining and decadent living

O n the threshold of the Peak District, in the old mining town of Bolsover, is this gem. It was built mostly by William Cavendish, the first Duke of Newcastle, a fine horseman - also fond of good living and earthly pleasures

Rise and fall

Bolsover castle is a semi ruined 17th century mansion on the site of a medieval castle. The castle was built by the Peverel family in the 12th century, (around the same time as William Peverel's other castle, at Castleton) and the community which is now Bolsover grew up around it. In 1155 the castle became crown property when Peverel fled to exile.

Tenants used the castle over the years and it was badly looked after, eventually ending up in ruins.

The neglected castle and its land was given by King Edward VI to Sir George Talbot, Sixth Earl of Shrewsbury, in 1553.

George is perhaps best known as the man who guarded Mary Queen of Scots whilst she was in captivity and also as being the husband of Bess of Hardwick. Bess already owned much land, including Chatsworth.

New plans

When the Earl died in 1590, Charles Cavendish, the son of Bess from an earlier marriage, leased and later bought the castle and started work on a new home on the site.

It is thought that Charles worked with the famous builder and designer Robert Smythson and came up with much of the concept, including the romantic design of the jewel box like Little Castle.

Both men, however, died before they had carried out many of their plans and it was their heirs who did more of the work at Bolsover.

Dreams and designs

The Little Castle

Venus fountain

The Terrace Range

The Stable

The Riding House

Entrance

PICTURE: By Roger Grayson, courtesy of the Derbyshire Times and The Chad

A pleasure palace

The castle that Charles had envisaged was for decadent living rather than defence. There is a lot of Italian influence in the design of the building, which adds elegance.

When Charles' son William took over the project, he incorporated his own indulgences into the design. including an entire block with riding house and stabling for his beloved horses.

Entering the castle today, by what was once the rear entrance, it is still most impressive. Even though some of it is in a ruinous state, it is easy to imagine how splendid it must have looked.

Walking around the stairs and corridors one can almost hear the music and the laughter, the chatter and murmurs of the past.

Recently there has been much restoration work to the castle and a new visitor centre added. The tower of the castle, now known as the Little Castle, is stunningly sumptuous, with wall panels and ceilings lovingly coaxed back to their former glory.

Views from the Terrace Range of the castle, left: out over the countryside and right: out to the Riding House range

The Riding School

The first block on the left as you enter the castle's great court is the Riding House Range. It was probably built in the 1630s, a huge block entirely devoted to care and use of horses, as William Cavendish was a passionate and dashing Cavalier.

William was well known for his skill as a horserider, writing books on the subject too. He even instructed royalty, having taught Prince Charles (later to become King Charles II) to ride.

The block has four parts. from the left was the forge area, then came the riding house, the stable and accommodation block.

The most impressive part is the riding house, which has a huge doorway to allow people to enter on horseback without dismounting. It is the best example in England still surviving. There are huge oak beams in the fine, high ceiling and there would have been soft sand on the floor for the horses hooves.. The room was not used to learn how to ride, but to show off the art of manège, which is making horses leap, kneel and circle.

In the 1660s, when William became too old to ride, he had a viewing gallery added so he could look down and watch the horsemanship.

The huge door of the riding school. Big enough to enter on horseback

In the stable block there is now a discovery centre, complete with a replica of the castle to explore

Above and below: The impressive Riding House, with its grand wooden roof

The Riding House was used as a set for the school in a TV production of Jane Eyre

The Terrace Range

The terrace. The staircase and entrance were the original way into Bolsover Castle. The doors in the building were aligned (see right) to show off the number of rooms

The Terrace Range was built in several stages over the second half of the 17th century. It was a huge project, built with the hopes of impressing the King and Queen, as William was hoping to get himself a royal position.

The range had an entrance hall, a great hall, a withdrawing room, lodging room, dressing room, long gallery and an impressive terrace tp parade and enjoy the views. The terrace and its grand staircase were the original entrance.

Improved, grand state rooms were added in the 1660s.

Now a roofless shell of its former glory but still an impressive building. It was not reduced to its ruinous state by Civil War action or attack, but because the family took most of the furnishings and fittings, including the lead roof, to their other and later more preferred home, at Welbeck.

From the terrace is a view over what was once the deerparks of the castle and also those of nearby Sutton (Scarsdale) Hall.

Today there are houses built for colliers and a motorway. But the view still conveys how impressive the castle would be, perched high on the hill.

The main doorway to the state rooms added in the 1660s

The Little Castle

This is the most unusual, and also the oldest, part of the castle. It is full of symbolic images, a place for pleasure and entertaining, with a jewel like variety of rooms full of colour and embellishments.

The building itself is romantic, like the notion of a miniature medieval castle from a fairytale. It is probably where the keep of the original Norman castle was, and is intentionally reminiscent of such a tower, with battlements, but was never intended for defensive purposes, just indulgent ones. There is an Italian style balcony, appearing to be held up by a statue of Hercules.

Hercules was a Greek hero who was famed for being able to subdue wild animals. He may also here be a symbol of the human trying to subdue the animal instincts within himself and arise to the more noble ones.

The dilemma of reconciling leisure and virtue was a popular concern at the time. Indeed the whole of the Little Castle is designed and decorated with this theme uppermost.

As you move through the Little Castle, you travel from earthly to heavenly themes, and each room is decorated with a specific aspect of human nature in mind.

The Heaven and Elysium rooms that lead off Williams's own bed-chamber are the end of the journey, and put forth these two themes of virtue and pleasure in the form of painted ceilings.

The heaven room illustrates spiritual concerns, with scenes from the life of Christ. The Elysium room, has Classical scenes of a pagan heaven of gods and goddesses. In the Elysium room, however, a painted banner gives a warning that 'All is but vanitie.'

Another lovely feature of the Little Castle is the octagonal lantern that lights the top storey of the house.

One of the gate posts at the entrance of the Little Castle

There are numerous rooms, all with their own charms. The Star Chamber, the great chamber of the castle, was only entered by the most privileged guests. Gold stars shine again from the sky blue ceiling, recreated to look as it would have when first painted.

The many fireplaces are works of art. The kitchens are fascinating too, with a worn step from the bustling staff as they went back and forth, having to cook and then carry the food up three staircases.

There is a large beer cellar that has a video about the castle. There is also a very well done and informative video of the Little Castle in the stables. There is no disabled access into this historic building, so the video is a good means of viewing the interior.

Details from the grand marble fireplaces. The dog below is from the Star Chamber fireplace, and is part of the Talbot coat of arms

Garden of delights

There is s walled garden around the Little Castle, with small fireplaces arranged in the perimeter wall. These would provide heat for the growing of fruits and vines. The plants in the garden today are all ones used in the seventeenth century, such as herbs and roses. The garden probably once thronged with people in their finery parading around and enjoying entertainments. Maybe the more daring ones even took a dip in the fountain.

Statues around the Venus fountain

The fountain

In the centre of the garden is an elaborate fountain, with a nude, thought to be Venus the goddess of love. The fountain has undergone considerable restoration in recent years and now the waters are playing again for the first time in two centuries.

Venus is surrounded by mythical beasts, some of whom are very well endowed so dont look too closely if you are easily embarrassed! These were newly carved, in the recent restoration, using drawings and fragments to get them as near to the originals as possible.

The fountain also has four boys relieving themselves, reconstructed from surviving fragments. The fountain, with its pagan theme, is appropriately overlooked from the balcony of the Elysium room.

New owners

After the Cavendish family had abandoned the site it eventually became home to the local vicar, Reverend John Hamilton Gray. and his wife. who leased the Little Castle in 1829.

They did a lot of work to make it into an acceptable country home after its sad neglect.

Gray did not approve of the erotic wall paintings in the Little Castle and swiftly covered them in whitewash. Little did he think that his handy work with a paintbrush would preserve them well to delight future generations!.

The vicar was perhaps more worldly and materialistic than the clergy were expected to be, and had many guests to show off his splendid home. It is thought it was some of these guests who left their mark in the form of drawing around their feet. Outlines of shoes were drawn on the lead roof of one of the courtyard lodges. An outline of a hand, dated 1839, was also left there.

Their landlord, the fourth Duke of Portland, repossessed the castle in 1849 and had a huge party there for his eighty-first birthday.

Bolsover was visited by Queen Mary in 1912. Later, during the First World War, the terrace Range was used as a rifle range. During the second World War, in 1945, the site was given over to the Ministry of Works and so to the nation, and opened to tourists.

By the 1970s it was in the care of English Heritage who began restoration. In the 1990s they undertook a huge programme of repairs and did sensitive restoration work.

Now the castle has new site interpretation facilities and a visitor centre, with books, including a good guide book. There are gifts to buy and a cafe. The castle looks better and brighter than it has for years and is a fascinating place to visit.

■ Bolsover Castle, Castle Street Bolsover, Derbyshire S44 6PR
■ Telephone: 01246 822844
■ www.english-heritage.org.uk
The interior of the Little Castle is not accessible for wheelchairs. Call or see website for entrance cost and opening times

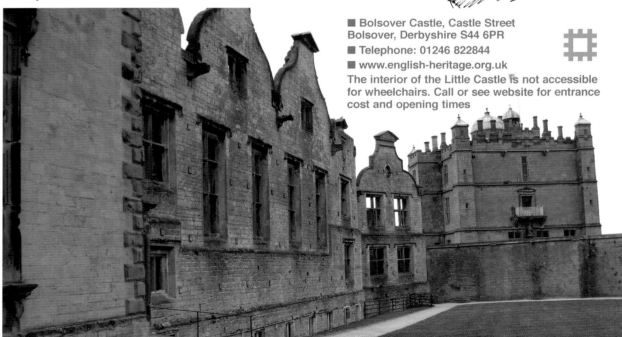

A perfect couple

William Cavendish

William was a very cultured man, with a love of music, literature, poetry, swordsmanship and horsemanship. He admired fine architecture too. He was considered to be a hedonist, enjoying the pleasurable things in life, and he freely spent his money on such things. He was very romantic, writing love poems to the two women he married in his lieftime. It seems he was quite a one for the ladies.

He was also known for his love of fine clothes and took quite a long time dressing, not too approved of when he was at war..

As well as writing books about horsemanship. he also wrote plays, some of which were performed in London.

His first wife was Elizabeth Bassett. whom he married in 1618. She died in 1643, when William was out of the country.

William was a Royalist leader in the Civil War, but he lost a key battle at Marston Moor in 1644. He then fled to the continent to avoid the Parliamentarians. One of the places he lived was in Antwerp, in the house of the painter Paul Rubens.

William met his second wife, Margaret, at the exiled court of Queen Henrietta Maria, in Paris.

Mad Madge

Margaret, whom William called Peg, sounds as amazing a character as her husband. She was very forward thinking and emancipated for her day. She wore men's clothes, published a book under her own name and was generally thought to behave outlandishly. She earned the nickname 'Mad Madge'.

Margaret would spend a lot of time in her closet, writing, which was unusual for a woman of the time. She penned a biography of William, as well as writings that bemoaned the role and lack of a proper education that was a woman's lot.

Love's welcome

William was always trying to impress the King and got his dream of entertaining the monarch, when King Charles visited Sherwood Forest in 1633 and stayed with William at his other home, Welbeck Abbey.

The king enjoyed himself so much that he came back a year later, this time with Queen Henrietta. Again the venue was Welbeck Abbey, and William left them to it - he stayed at Bolsover Castle.

William put on a grand evening's entertainment for the royal couple, at Bolsover, on July 13th, 1634. To make it a grand occasion, William invited all the gentry he knew, and also asked his friend, the poet and playwright Ben Jonson, to write a masque especially for the event.

The masque was called Love's Welcome and was performed in various parts of the castle, in between dancing, speeches and a series of banquets with lots of extravagant eating!

The menu probably looked similar to a list of the inhabitants of a zoo or wildlife park, with peacocks, swans and sturgeons on the menu.

One of the banquets was 'set downe from the cloudes' by two cupids. This may have been some kind of mechanical lowering of the food by people dressed as cupids, perhaps from the Elysium room balcony, and was designed to impress the royals.

These two cupids then spoke of what a perfect and loving couple William and Margaret were - great propaganda to try and convince the king that he was a good man to have at the royal court.

All this fine entertaining came at a great price and left William deeply in debt. The cost was almost £15,000, a huge amount even by today's standards.

And after all that he still didn't get his royal commission.

The couple certainly seemed to have been devoted to and fascinated by each other. Margaret's biography gives a very affectionate portrait of William. Bolsover's Little Castle and the romantic, sensual nature of the decorations and gardens must have been an ideal setting for this unusual pair- their very own pleasure palace.

Cavorting cherubs from the Elysium Room ceiling

He did however, get the rank of Duke bestowed on him in 1665, when King Charles II was invited back to England after Oliver Cromwell's death, and did not forget his old tutor. It was when he got this title that William did a lot more building at Bolsover, including new state rooms on the Terrace Range and the revamping of the Riding School.

A Loyal Duke

William seemed to retain his sense of showmanship even down to the time of his death - on Christmas Day, in 1676.

He was buried in Westminster Abbey, under a tomb marked 'The Loyall Duke.'

After the death of William, the castle eventually passed, by marriage, into the ownership of the Dukes of Portland. It remained in their hands until being given to the nation in 1945.

The Cundy House

The Cundy House is a small conduit house built in the seventeenth century to provide a water supply to the nearby Bolsover Castle. It stands at the junction of Craggs Road and Houghton Road in Bolsover and has been recently restored, including having a new vaulted stone-slab roof fitted.

In the 1970's, it was a roofless ruin and became a target for vandalism and misuse. Detailed investigation revealed that the building at one time would have had a solid stone-vaulted roof on top of an arched vault This roof was recreated with timber supports in 2002-2003, when gable stone work had to be rebuilt and the stone slabs fixed, all worked out according to the remains that were left.

All the stone used for the work is local, being magnesian limestone from Bolsover Moor Quarry.

Over 50 tons of masonry was re-fixed and the building was also given an iron grille door and a path leading up to it.

Visitors can see the remains of the original brick water tank inside through the iron grille door.

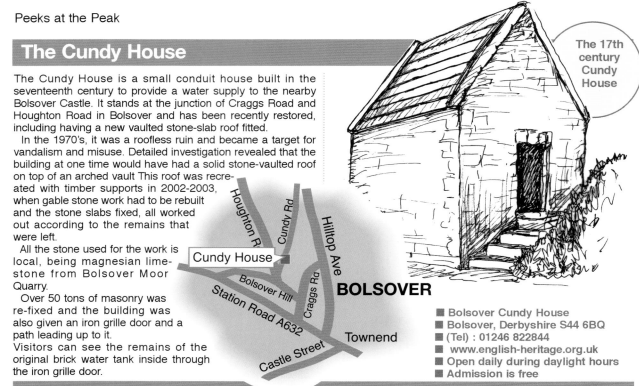

The 17th century Cundy House

Cundy House

BOLSOVER

Townend

- Bolsover Cundy House
- Bolsover, Derbyshire S44 6BQ
- (Tel) : 01246 822844
- www.english-heritage.org.uk
- Open daily during daylight hours
- Admission is free

Sutton Scarsdale Hall

Not far from Bolsover and three miles from Chesterfield is what was once another great and opulent hall. Now an evocative ruin, Sutton Scarsdale Hall would once have rivalled Chatsworth, but now looks across to Bolsover Castle on the hillside opposite as a shadow of its former grand self.

This was not the first hall to be built on the site, and could possibly be the fourth or fifth. The present, now ruined, hall is modelled from an earlier building of 1724. The architect Francis Smith of Warwick did the work for Nicholas Leke, the fourth and last Earl of Scarsdale and used materials from the older hall for new one. The Coat of Arms of the Earls of Scarsdale still survives on the central pediment.

The interior had fine plasterwork by Atari and Vassali, and huge carved marble fireplaces and ornate oak staircases. Outside were splendid formal gardens.

In the Civil War the older hall on the site was a Royalist stronghold, as the Leke family were staunch Royalists. When the Civil War broke out it was fortified to defend it from attacks by the Parliamentarians. Even so, the house was stormed and its defences removed.

The hall though, stayed in the Leke family. In 1724 when Earl Nicholas did all the rebuilding, he got badly in debt and sold the hall in 1740 to Godfrey Clarke of Somershall.

It eventually came into the hands of the son of Richard Arkwright of Cromford Mill. The estate remained in their family until 1919, when it was sold at auction.

The hall was neglected and fell into disrepair. A group of Chesterfield business men bought it, but it was so ruinous they decided not to do anything with it but dismantle it and sell off the contents, including the lead roof. This meant the place deteriorated further and more quickly.

In 1946 Sir Osbert Sitwell of Renishaw Hall heard that it was to be demolished to re-use the stone and stepped in to save it. Though by then it was just a shell, he wanted to preserve the remains as an atmospheric ruin.

The Sitwell family held it till 1970s then persuaded the government to have it for nation. Now it is cared for by English Heritage and freely accessible.

Film-star fittings

English Heritage tracked down what happened to some of the interior fittings and furnishings of the hall after they had been sold in 1919. Panelled wall fittings are now in the Philadelphia Museum of Art in America. (www.philamuseum.org) The museum bought three rooms to display english paintings in, the reception room and two others. The panels were adapted to fit their new home so do not look same as when at Sutton Scarsdale.

A room called the No 4 Pine Room was purchased by American newspaper baron Randolph Hearst. He was the man whom Citizen Kane was based on and so wonderfully filmed by Orson Wells. Hearst never managed to use his purchase as he became short of cash and sold it. Paramount film studios bought it and in 1945 they used it as a set for a film called Kitty, starring Ray Miland and Paulette Goddard. This was a Pygmalion-like story of a poor girl who ends up as a model for the painter Gainsborough.

According to the Hal Erickson All Movies Net Guide website, it was then used again in a film, this time Monsieur Beauclaire, starring Bob Hope, in 1946.

After this it was bought by The Huntingdon Library, a museum in Pasedena Los Angeles, to be used a s boardroom. It didnt fit - and now most of it is in storage, though two door cases were fitted into an office there.

Edale & Kinder Scout

The village of Edale sits amongst stunning scenery, with Kinder Scout and Mam Tor for companions

Popular pubs in Edale - The Old Nags Head and The Rambler

Edale is well known in walking circles for two things, being the start of the Pennine Way and being close to the scene of a mass trespass on Kinder Scout.

The place is also a favourite camping spot, with inspiring scenery, good pubs and a prestigious information and research centre.

The village

The village of Edale consists of five hamlets or booths : Barber Booth, Grindsbrook Booth, Ollerbrook Booth, Upper Booth and Nether Booth. It sits in a wide valley through which runs the River Noe. The more central booth is Grindsbrook Booth, which is the part most people call or think of as Edale Village.

.The place is long established and is mentioned in the Domesday book as Aidele. The parish church, the third on the site, was built in 1886.

Connections

The railway arrived at Edale in 1894. Until then the village was quite an isolated spot. The Totley Tunnel opened up the route between Manchester and Sheffield. This created more village growth and also saw many walkers from the cities coming by train to enjoy the area.

The Pennine Way starts from the village square.in front of the Old Nags Head public house. Kinder Scout is also a popular and spectacular walking spot.

Edale Parish Church

Scenery when walking out from Edale towards Mam Tor

Peat cutting and erosion

Peat is formed, over a long time, from decomposing vegetable matter. It makes a good fuel, so was used for lead smelting and lime burning. Kiln dried wood, known as whitecoal, could also be used for the fuel. Early lead smelting took place on bole hearths, placed on ridgetops and high hills to take advantage of the winds to create a good draught. This would get the fire up to a high enough temperature. Later the smelting was done in ore hearths, that used water power to drive bellows to create a draught, so smelt sites moved down to valleys, by rivers.

From around the mid 17th century the method changed again and the cupola was developed. These used coal to fuel furnaces. Building of canals made coal easier to get as did road building. Even with coal easier to get, peat was still cut for domestic fuel. Landowners gave the right to cut peat to people. This right is known as turbary. Peat pits were sited on Crookstone Moor, below Ringing Roger and at Grindlow, all on Kinder Scout. The peat was cut and then brought down from the moors on horse drawn sledges. The blocks were called 'peats'. As they were cut they were stacked, propped one against the other, in 'footings' to dry. On the last day of cutting the footings were stacked into piles called 'pikes'. Gaps were left for the wind to blow through. The blocks would get smaller and harder as they dried.

Peat is still used as domestic fuel in some places today, but is seen by most of us bagged up in garden centres as compost. There is a movement to replace the peat with other products, as peat erosion is a great cause for concern and we need to conserve the peat deposits that are left.

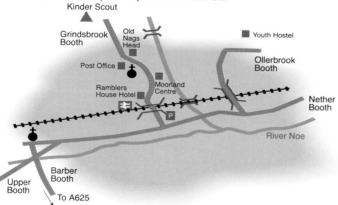

Helicopters to fly heather for moors

By Bill Brotherton

HELICOPTERS will be airlifting heather on to moorland next summer to regenerate vegetation and wildlife on Kinder Scout.

Work to to keep heather growing on the moors will go ahead thanks to a £500,000 sponsorship deal announced by British Gas for the National Trust.

The Trust's High Peak Estate is to get £12,000 a year to ensure the plant — which is vital to vegetation on Kinder

Acid rain, fires, heather burning on grouse moors, overgrazing and walkers have damaged the peat deposits over a wider area than peat cutting and has put environmental pressure on areas such as Kinder. When the peat goes, plants don't grow, then plant roots don't hold the remaining peat and it washes away more easily. A circular problem.

As well as this, healthy peat is able to absorb excess carbon dioxide in the atmosphere, but degraded peat doesn't do this and so the carbon dioxide is not absorbed, or is even released and this adds to climate change problems.

There have been many campaigns and efforts to try and reduce the peat erosion on Kinder Scout with large scale planting of heather and cotton grass. The roots of these plants stabilise the soil and the tops protect the soil from the elements.

Luckily there are now many alternatives to buying peat for our gardens at the expense of the wilder places.

Grindsbrook House in Edale. There was once a lot of peat cutting on the land around here

The Moorland Centre

Built on the site of the former Fieldhead Centre, this striking building is an information centre, learning facility and research base. It was opened in 2006 by the Duke of Devonshire.

The roof is covered in sedum turf and has running water over glass panels. which falls into a pool at the front of the building. It is heated by a ground source heat pump.

There are interactive exhibitions, books, gifts and information on accommodation, events and much more. A covered walkway to a refurbished farmhouse links the centre to the research base, home to the Moors for the Future team.

The centre is surrounded by the Fieldhead camp site. There is no public car park, to encourage the use of public transport.

■ The Moorland Centre, Fieldhead, Edale, Hope Valley S33 7ZA   ■ Telephone: 01433 670207
■ email: edale@peakdistrict.gov.uk

You may hear the haunting cry of a Curlew

A curious sheep near Grindsbrook Booth, with the moorland spreading behind

A forbidding mountain

Kinder Scout is a high and windswept gritstone plateau, one of the most forbidding places in the Dark Peak. The highest point is Crowden Head, 636 metres (2,088ft) above sea level, also the highest point in the Peak District. The weather can change from bright sunshine to mist in a few minutes and anyone venturing there is advised to be well equipped and also use a compass.

There is some spectacular scenery, including the Kinder Downfall waterfall, a reservoir, and interesting rock formations. Edale, up Grindsbrook or Jacob's Ladder, or Hayfield, up William Clough, are the most used access points onto the plateau.

Being the highest point in the area, with jagged outcrops and rapidly changing weather, it is no surprise that Kinder has claimed the lives of aircraft crew over the years. Many planes became victims of the terrain in the second World War.

One such plane, whose crew luckily survived, was on a routine map reading exercise in December 1945. The RAF Twin-engined Airspeed Oxford training aircraft crashed in thick cloud into an area called Brown Knoll.

Sheffield Star, January 1983

Pilot's agony crawl to rescue mates

AIR VICTIMS OF MOORS

A STRANGE and frightening sight greeted a Derbyshire woman when she answered the knock at the door of her isolated farm cottage.

Crouched on the doorstep in the half-light of dusk was the bedraggled figure of a Royal Air Force pilot, his clothing soaked and torn, who gasped out his story after being helped shivering to the fireside.

By Paul Allonby

FLASHBACK — an air crash on Kinder Scout, 1963

Soccer's Ted Croker — former RAF officer

PHOTO: Sheffield Newspapers Archives

Rescue of the aircrew from Kinder, Dec 1945

Ted Croker, George Robinson and John Dowthwaite
PHOTOS: Sheffield Newspapers Archives

Least injured crew member. Flying Officer Ted Croker, wrapped the other two men in their parachutes to keep them warm, then crawled on hands and knees, with both ankles broken, to the nearest isolated cottage a mile or so outside Edale. Men from the then newly formed Mountain Rescue team began a search. After 20 hours the injured airmen, John Dowthwaite of Bradford and George Robinson of Richmond, Sheffield, were carried to safety.

In 1985 the three airmen made an emotional return to the site of the crash. They had last met when in hospital in 1946 recovering from their injuries and had been brought together by author Ron Collier of Glossop, author of the book Dark Peak Aircraft wrecks. The men drank champagne at the site.

The warden service

The 1949 National Parks and Access To the Countryside Act made provision for the appointment of countryside wardens. These wardens were to help the public and to make sure any bye laws relating to land and access were adhered to.

The warden service actually started in January 1954, when the first national park warden in the country, Tom Tomlinson, was appointed.

On Good Friday of the same year, the Peak District National Park Voluntary Warden Service was inaugurated outside the Old Nags Head Inn in Edale.

In 1958 a warden course started at Edale for a more formal sort of training, and the service kept expanding, with some paid posts becoming part of the service.

By the 1960s the wardens had their own meeting place, at Fieldhead House, with an Information Centre. This site is where the Moorland Centre now stands.

The warden or Ranger service has grown over the years. Rangers help with many varied tasks, such as guided walks, outdoor activities, conservation work, practical work such as mending stiles, helping residents, farmers and landowners, community projects, and giving many visitors and students environmental information and advice.

These services are a vital part of life in the Peak District and help the thousands of people who come to enjoy it do so more fully and safely.

Warden Service Starts

3,400 Acres More For Ramblers Shortly?

TO the 6,000 acres already made available to the public in the Kinder Scout area of the Peak District National Park since 1949, it is hoped to add a further 3,400 acres "within days."

Coun. J. M. Roberts, chairman of the Access and Finance committees of the Peak Planning Board, said this yesterday when the warden service was inaugurated at a ceremony outside the Nag's Head, Edale.

He said it was the board's intention to get for the public within the next 12 months if possible access to 27 square miles of the Kinder Scout area.

Inaugurating the service, Ald. C. F. White, chairman of the board, and of the Derbyshire County Council, told a large body of ramblers who were present: "To my mind we are, this Good Friday morning, really opening this great national park."

First Briefing

Speaking into a B.B.C. microphone, and with a television newsreel camera trained on him, Ald. White continued: "I am very proud to be the chairman of the authority which since 1949 has

THE HEAD WARDEN, Mr. T. D. Tomlinson, pointing out the routes over Kinder Scout to the rest of the wardens yesterday. BELOW: Conn. Mrs. Eileen Daley, of Marple, Cheshire, the only woman warden.

"Inside the Nags Head the ten men and one woman team of ramblers received their first briefing from the head warden Mr Tom D Tomlinson, who pointed out the 10-15 mile a day weekend patrols they would do. "

Sheffield Telegraph, April 17th 1954

The Kinder Mass Trespass

PHOTO: Sheffield Newspapers Archives

Benny Rothman speaking in the quarry in 1932

April 24 1932

In the depression of the 1930s, there was mass unemployment. Many working class people, with little funds, gained pleasure from the free and healthy activity of 'rambling' or walking in the countryside as a release from worry and the confines of the city. Leaving from Manchester and Sheffield, hundreds of people spent their sundays, the only day off work for many, in the hills and dales.

However a lot of moorland was kept for grouse shooting and no one was allowed across it. The land was not used a lot the rest of year. The walkers wanted public paths, so they could walk there when the land was not in use.
As landowners were seen as wealthy, many of the protesters saw this right to roam as a class issue too.

The matter came to a head in April 1932, in what became known as the Mass Trespass, on Kinder Scout.

A few weeks before this, frustrated walkers, members of the British Workers' Sports Federation, were turned off by gamekeepers at Bleaklow. The idea of a mass trespass started because they thought that if there had been more of them instead of six or seven they wouldn't have been turned off so easily.

On Sunday 24 April 1932, about 400 (reports vary) ramblers walked from Hayfield, up William Clough towards Kinder Scout.

Some of the official rambling groups heard about the plan and didn't approve. Police had heard of the plans and were in the area at Hayfield. They let the ramblers assemble but then moved them on. The ramblers were undeterred and re-formed at Bowden Bridge Quarry.

The trespassers were led by a man called Benny Rothman. He and others were members or supporters of the Young Communist League in Manchester. He spoke at the quarry.

Punctually at two o'clock the ramblers who had gathered there set off for Kinder. At a whistle signal, they left the track and headed up onto the forbidden plateau of Kinder.

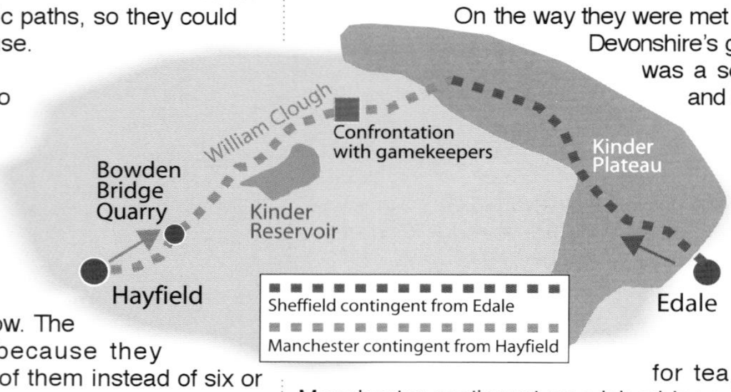

On the way they were met by some of the Duke of Devonshire's gamekeepers and there was a scuffle. One keeper fell and sprained his ankle.

The ramblers continued along the hillside towards Ashop Head, the summit of the public footpath from Hayfield to the Snake Inn on the Glossop-Sheffield Road. There was a halt for tea, and then this large Manchester contingent was joined by a party of about 30 from Sheffield, who had marched from Hope and up from Edale over Jacob's Ladder. There were some speeches then they marched back down to Hayfield and Edale.

Map labels: William Clough · Bowden Bridge Quarry · Kinder Reservoir · Hayfield · Confrontation with gamekeepers · Kinder Plateau · Edale · Sheffield contingent from Edale · Manchester contingent from Hayfield

Imprisonment

At Hayfield, the returning ramblers found that the keeper who had hurt his ankle had told the police he had been assaulted and six of the trespassers were arrested.

Rothman and four others were charged with "riotous assembly". One man, said to have hurt the gamekeeper, was charged with grievous bodily harm but maintained he was innocent. Four of the six were found guilty at a trial at Derby Assizes and jailed for between two and six months.

The jury was made up mainly of country gentlemen, who people thought were unsympathetic to the politics of the men on trial. The sentences were seen by many as too harsh and within weeks around 10,000 people demonstrated at an access rally at Winnats Pass in Castleton. This wave of public sympathy helped the cause for the right to roam. Before this day, no direct action had attracted the general public's attention so successfully.

HEFFIELD DAILY TELEGRAPH. MONDAY, APRIL 25. 1932.

RKABLE POLL IN PRUSSI

ON KINDER.—The struggle between combined Sheffield and Manchester ramblers and gamekeepers yesterday, in which one keeper (seen on right) was injured.

Report of the incident the day after, in the Sheffield Daily Telegraph

48

A long time coming

The second World War interrupted any further developments and it was another 17 years before any changes were made, when Parliament passed the National Parks and Access To the Countryside Act in 1949.

The Peak District National Park was created in 1951 and negotiations led to an agreement of access on parts of Kinder in 1953. More access was granted in 1955 and 1957.

The Countryside and Rights of Way Act 2000 with final implementation in 2004/ 5, meant even more access.. The act enshrines the right to walk across "mountain, moor, heath and downland", in addition to other areas to which the public already has right of way.

An iconic event

The Mass Trespass has become a legend in the fight for access and, as with most legends, the facts have been disputed. The number of walkers and gamekeepers said to have been involved has varied wildly, as has the distance of the trespass itself.

Whatever the truth, the event is now seen as a major factor in helping get the rights to roam and the creation of National Parks.

Remembered in song

A favourite song lustily sung in many a bar or on a group walk is one by folk singer Ewan MacColl (father of Kirsty). He wrote his classic ballad The Manchester Rambler, in honour of the Kinder Mass Trespass..

MacColl (1915-1989) was born in Salford. He was a Member of The Young Communist League. He was passionate about theatre and rambling and was a member of the British Workers Sports Federation. He was one of the people involved in the mass trespass and his song was inspired by it.

Plaque placed at Bowden Bridge Quarry in 1982

The words of the song reflect his love of the countryside and mention many of the places associated with the trespass. Here is an extract and the well known chorus:

I've been over Snowdon, I've slept upon Crowden,
I've camped by the Wain Stones as well;
I've sunbathed on Kinder, been burned to a cinder,
And many more things I can tell;
My rucksack has oft been my pillow.
The heather has oft been my bed;
And sooner than part from the mountains,
I think I would rather be dead.

Chorus
I'm a rambler, I'm a rambler from Manchester way,
I get all my pleasure the hard moorland way;
I may be a wage slave on Monday,
but I am a free man on Sunday.

Remembering the Mass Trespass

At the 50th anniversary of the mass trespass in 1982, more than 2000 ramblers took part, including Benny Rothman and others of the original trespassers of 1932. The day began with the unveiling of a plaque at Bowden Bridge Quarry, the starting point of the mass trespass, unveiled by John Beadle, then chairman of the Peak Park Planning board.

Benny Rothman died at the age of 91 in 2002, two years after the passing of the Countryside and Rights of Way Act, which gave ramblers the right of access to mountain and moorland in England and Wales.

A day of music and song celebrated the 70th anniversary of the Mass Trespass, on April 27 2002.

Also the then 11th Duke of Devonshire apologised for his grandfather's actions at the event of 1932..

PHOTOS: Sheffield Newspapers Archives

Left: Benny Rothman speaking in the quarry in 1982 and (above) heading the crowd of walkers

Evocative traces and phantoms

PICTURE: Courtesy of Dr David Clarke, from his book Supernatural Peak District

Wreckage of a US Air Force B29 Superfortress plane on Bleaklow. Thirteen air crew died in the crash, in 1948. The site is said to be haunted by the ghost of an airman in full flying uniform

The Peak District has many aircraft wreck sites, some with traces of the aircraft still scattered like metal bones over the moors. They are sobering places, where men met their deaths, or made lucky escapes in hard and frightening circumstances.

Some, like the site of the wreck of a US Airforce Superfortress plane on Bleaklow, pictured above, have become places where the brave fliers are remembered by a memorial and an annual service.

The Superfortress site is a particularly evocative one, and there are tales of people seeing ghostly airmen in the area, in full flying uniform.

Over the years some of the wreck debris of the various crash sites has been taken by souvenir hunters, some has been buried by the passage of time. But time does not seem to have dimmed the effect the sites have on people. Neither does it seem to have lessened the reports of old wartime planes seen still flying the Peak District's skies - this time not crashing, but quietly disappearing into thin air. Many sightings of phantom planes have been reported, with the viewers so convinced that they called up the emergency services because they were sure there had been a crash. After searches, nothing was ever found.

No old planes still in existence were flying at the time of the sightings, so the explanation is still a mystery.

Dr. David Clarke, an expert in folklore, strange events and urban myths, spoke with many people who said they saw such planes, and writes about the subject in his book, Supernatural Peak District. He tells of people seeing in 1995 a 'huge old plane' with propellers flying silently over Grindleford and disappearing, of phantom Lancasters seen skimming the waters of Ladybower Reservoir and of ghostly airmen wandering in the mists.

Whatever the truth of these sightings, they are a testament to the enduring power that the events of the war and it's casualties has on the Peak, its visitors and residents..

Misty views of Edale. It is easy to imagine restless ghosts still walk the hills

Hannah Mitchell

Alport Castles. with the farm where Hannah Mitchell grew up in the background

PHOTOGRAPH: Trevor Prew

The landscape off the A57 Snake Pass is still some of the wildest in the Peak. It was home to Hannah Mitchell, who, with only two weeks schooling, grew up to be a fighter for women's' rights, a councillor and a magistrate.

Alport Castles

Alport Castles is a millstone grit feature, where a landslide has left towers that do indeed look like castles.

Hannah Maria Webster was born at Alport Castle Farm in 1871. The daughter of John Webster, a Derbyshire farmer and his wife Ann. The farm stands in an area known as The Woodlands.

A hard childhood

In later years, Hannah wrote her autobiography, which gives a fascinating glimpse into the times and struggles.

Her parents had always been hardworking and struggling to make ends meet. Her mother was in service when she met the man she later married. After they wed they took on the job of looking after the toll-bar on the Manchester to Sheffield Road (now the A57).

When the tolls were abolished they took on the farm at Alport Castles. They were still poor and took on the farm with borrowed money, which they were always struggling to pay back.

They had six children, Hannah was the fourth and had three brothers and two sisters. Hannah's parents had the larger of two small farms. The other was kept by a widow and her two daughters. Hannah described the farm in her book....

"Two farms hidden away in the wildest part of the Derbyshire moorlands. Originally there were three, one large, two small, forming a small hamlet, a good mile from the turnpike, as the dalesfolk call the high road."

Later the family took over the smaller farm too and it was rebuilt by the Cavendish Estate, to whom the estate belonged.

"The roof had been raised and new inner walls built. A new dairy was built behind the kitchen, this was a big and airy place with stone benches all around, on which the pans of milk were set to cool."

Hannah's mother seemed unhappy in the countryside, but Hannah loved it there:

"I loved the hills, loved to listen at night to the rushing mountain streams"

she could *"respond to the beauty of a field of golden buttercups, hunt the hedgerows for wild violets, or climb the great tor for the primroses which grew in sheltered nooks."*

Hannah Mitchell in 1924, based on a photograph in her auto-biography

A hard life

At the farm there were many domestic tasks which fell to Hannah and her sisters, though not to her brothers, which fed her beliefs that the lot for women should be a lot more equal:

"I think my first reactions to feminism began at this time when I was forced to darn my brothers' stockings while they read or played cards or dominoes..... the fact that the boys could read if they wished filled my cup with bitterness to the brim."

Hannah and her siblings had all been taught to read by their father and uncle. The girls however, had to borrow books from their brothers and had no leisure time to indulge.

The boys also got to got to school. After crying for the same privilege, Hannah and her sister Lizzie were allowed to go too.

But the school was a long way off and the winter came, so after just two weeks, school was abandoned and they were kept home.

In the spring, Hannah was terribly disappointed as her sister was alowed back to school in the town ten miles away, but she was made to stay at home and do chores.

After school her sister stayed on in the town with a job as a dressmaker, but Hannah was still a drudge, at the farm.

One day a passing walker who called at the farm for refreshment cheered her up by giving her a book of Wordsworth's poems. She was thirsty for knowledge, but she had hardly had any reading material so getting a book was a real treat.

Escape

Hannah never fitted into the accepted role at home, She hated housework and cooking. This did not help the relationship between her and her mother, who, as well as having a bad and unpredictable temper, had an obsession for housework which her daughter did not share:

"sometimes carrying her love of cleanliness to the point of absurdity, as for instance when she used her leftover soap suds on washing days to scrub and wash the pigs."

Hannah could not take it any more and, at just 14 years old, she ran away from home, determined to earn a living away from all the housework.

Work and Labour

But work elsewhere was still a drudge. Hannah made ends meet by taking low paid jobs, ironically at first as a maid, but then as a dressmaker. Another position she took was as a dressmaker, in Bolton. Here she made wedding and bridesmaids dresses, for just 10 shillings (50p) a week:

"No talking was allowed and although we often worked late, we were fined a penny for every five minutes we were late."

The hard work and unfair treatment made Hannah well aware of the fight for better working conditions.

Though it was hard, Hannah valued her independence and was quite scathing of others she knew who had got married instead, as well as the men they had chosen:

"Several girlfriends had fallen victims to the primitive passions of the farm lads, who in many cases were scarcely more intelligent and not so decent as the animals they tended."

From these comments it is easy to see why some thought Hannah quite abrasive, but she was also witty and had the nickname of 'Miss Repartee.'

Marriage

Hannah managed to find work at a dressmaking firm in Bolton. where she met a man who did meet with her approval. He was a staunch Socialist named Gibbon Mitchell. She began attending meetings with him at the Bolton branch of the Independent Labour Party, became active in the trade union movement and subscribed to their journal, The Clarion.

Hannah Mitchell in later years, with one of the banners

PHOTOGRAPH: Manchester Archives & Local Studies, Central Library

[Map labels:] Glossop · Howden Reservoir · Alport Castles Farm · Derwent Reservoir · To Manchester · Alport Castles · Ladybower Reservoir · A57 · Kinder Scout · To Sheffield · A57 · Edale · A625 · A625 · Castleton

Rights and Suffrage

Hannah and Gibbon got married in 1895. Hannah insisted that they should share the domestic duties, but the reality of married life and hoped for equality seemed to fall a little short::

"I soon found that a lot of the Socialist talk about freedom was only talk and these Socialist young men expected Sunday dinners and huge teas with home-made cakes, potted meat and pies and the like."

Hannah and Gibbon had one child, a son called Frank, though she hardly mentions him in her auto-biography.

The family moved to Newhall in South Derbyshire as Gibbon had got a job in a tailors there. They also were involved with the 'Clarion Van.' The Clarion was the new magazine of the Socialists and the van was a way of spreading the socialist message. The horse drawn 'van' was fitted up with beds, a stove and a few cooking utensils.

This life went happily enough, but Hannah couldn't settle in Newhall and longed to move somewhere a little wilder again.

"I had been raised in the shadow of Kinder Scout, the wildest part of The Peak of Derbyshire, where winter lasts half the year and the wind blows sear from the hills."

In 1900, they moved to Ashton-under-Lyne, when Gibbon got a job at the Co-Operative tailoring Department.

This move may have suited Hannah better as far as locality went, but she was still finding married life itself had to adjust to and maybe understood why her mother had been so bad tempered about things. The everyday routine was a depressing restriction to Hannah and, as today, many people will perhaps agree with her words as they balance life, home and family as she was doing:

"The tyranny of meals is the worst snag in the house-wife's lot. Her life is bounded on the north by breakfast, south by dinner, east by tea and in the west by supper and the most sympathetic man can never be made to understand that meals do not come up through the tablecloth, but have to be planned, bought and cooked."

Women's rights

The feelings Hannah had always had about equality and women's right found a natural outlet and cause in the Suffragette movement. In 1904 Hannah joined the Women's Social and Political Union (WSPU), which was started by Mrs Pankhurst. Her husband supported her and acted as her body-guard at public meetings.

She became known as a good speaker and would often be banner waving:

"We became quite adept as making our own little banners, a square of white calico with the slogan 'Votes For Women' painted on with black enamel. We always took several, as they were often snatched from us and we had to fight hard to retain one of them."

She was imprisoned in Strangeways with other suffragettes in 1906, for obstruction and non-payment of fines.

Though dedicated, Hannah became dissatisfied with the way that the Pankhurst's dominated the movement. She also did not like the increasing attacks of arson that the WSPU were involved with, and in 1907 she joined instead the Women's Freedom League, with it's pacifist ideals, and later refused to help in the WSPU's recruiting campaign for the war in 1914. Instead she joined the Independent Labour Party and opposed the war.

A Political Life

Hannah's was later elected to the Manchester City Council, in 1924 and by 1926 was a Magistrate. She retired from the Council in 1935, after an active life there, which also included initiating many worthwhile schemes such as wash houses and travelling libraries.

Reminders

Hannah recorded her life in her auto-biography 'The Hard Way Up':

"most of it was written during the war with the drone of aircraft overhead and guns roaring out their challenge."

She died in 1956 and the book was published after her death.

There is a plaque (right) at Hannah's old home at 43 Elizabeth Street in Ashton under Lyne, where they lived from 1900-1910.

The last words of her book sum up her enjoyment of life and her hopes that her cause will be carried on:

"Life to me has been a great adventure, a wonderful thing rounding itself off with time to sit back and rest. The work we began, the cause we sponsored, the faith we held will all remain to be carried on, we hope, by abler hands than ours."

The Alport Love Feast

A great feature of Hannah's life was the annual Love Feast, held in high summer in her father's barn. Hannah came back every year to her childhood home to attend this event.

The Love Feast is a simple ceremony to commemorate the fact that over 300 years ago, non-conformists met to worship in secret. The gathering for the feast was a grand occasion and a welcome disruption in daily life at the farm for Hannah. The house was cleaned and the family fed the hoards of visitor's breakfast.

"At one o'clock the Lovefeast began with the singing of a hymn, 'Jesu lover of my soul' being the favourite and prayer followed by the breaking of bread."

Methodist worshippers keep the tradition alive with a meal there still, every year on the first Sunday in July, at 1.30pm.

Hannah called the feast one of the year's 'two red letter days'. The other one was the hiring fair at Hope, six miles away. At the fair, people looking for work would come in search of jobs.

"Youths and maidens wishing to 'better themselves' by a change of situation arrived in the village, grouping themselves by the churchyard railings."

The day was turned into a big event, with stalls, games and dancing and inns put on special fair day meals of roast beef and plum pudding.

Treats of nuts and gingerbread, ribbons and beads were bought and later there was dancing and gameplaying until dusk. It is easy to see why the event held a strong place in the heart of a child as a highlight of the year.

Some wild flowers

A few of the common flowers you may spot on your walks

HAREBELLS: Common plant on dry heath and grassland. Flowers July to october

BINDWEED: Found in hedges and bushy places. Large white flowers July/August

LESSER CELANDINE: One of the earliest spring flowers, from end of January

LORDS AND LADIES: Found in woods and shady hedge banks

STITCHWORT: A common flower in spring woodlands and hedgerows

YELLOW ARCHANGEL: Common in woody areas in May and June

RAMSONS: Wild garlic, appearing in woods and shady places April - June

WOOD SORREL: White bell-like flowers and trefoil leaves. Flowers April - May

DOG VIOLET: Found in woods and grassy places from March to May

Dronfield Church

John the Baptist is the saint who gives his name to this fine old building

The church of St John the Baptist, Dronfield, stands proudly in an elevated spot overlooking the River Drone, as it has done throughout the centuries. The earliest known date for this fine church is 1135, when the rector was a man called Oscot.

Wool, dyes and scythes

From 1260 to 1399 the patronage of the parish was with a family named Brailsford. They sold the living to Beauchief Abbey, which is only about three miles away. The Canons from the abbey then controlled the church for over 130 years, until the Reformation.

The grand church reflects the fact that it was quite a wealthy parish. This was because Dronfield was on the lead and grindstone making routes and people would have passed through or stayed there a lot and also wealthy lead merchants made their homes there.

The wool trade was also a means of income, with farmers, spinners and weavers working in the area. A dye works used for the resulting cloth once stood on Soaper Lane. As suggested by the name, soap making and tanning were also trades found in this river area. Scythe making was also carried out in Dronfield.

The church exterior

Traces of old roof lines, like ghosts of the older building, can be spotted as you look at the exterior of the church today.

The tower was added in 1360, with the upper part being completed in 1405. It had to be rebuilt in 1818 when it was struck by lightning and collapsed. The roof and walls were also damaged by the fall and repaired then. There are eight bells in the tower, plus a Sanctus bell.

To the left as you enter the lych gate is a memorial garden. The graveyard is now closed to burials, but many people have their ashes put in this pretty place.

Also in the churchyard are what are thought to be the remains of an old preaching cross, which probably predated the church. The stump is all that is left now, but it would have once been much taller and a focus of community worship.

The Green Dragon Inn, opposite the main gate of the church, is traditionally thought to be the old dwelling of the chantry priests. These priests had the role of praying for the souls of the dead at the church.

One of the carvings from the choir stalls

Inside the inn are remains of the old building, including parts of the kitchen - and there is rumoured to be a tunnel under it leading to the church.

Perhaps the old chantry was turned into an inn after the Dissolution of the Monasteries.

Next to the inn is the Chantry Hotel, which suggests this was once part of the same building.

Inside the church

Venturing into the church interior reveals some lovely architectural features and carvings. The nave is one of the oldest parts of the church. The south aisle was added around 1200 and the north about 1405.

The 1135 nave roof was also raised to a higher level then and clerestory windows added.

There was also a lot more rebuilding work during the thirteenth, fourteenth and fifteenth centuries, including the large chancel. Some of the roof timbers are thought to be around 600 years old.

Some features

The church font is a simple octagon shape and was recovered after being found in the garden of the old vicarage. It could be from as early as the fourteenth century. Now it stands solidly on a modern base, made for it in 1917.

The pulpit is from around 1603 and covered in Tudor designs. It used to be higher but was lowered in 1917. A wrought iron staircase leads up to it.

Above the pulpit is a door that seems to open into mid air, but would once have led onto a platform above the rood (cross) screen.

A sleeping figure carved from alabaster is thought to be an effigy of a man named Sir Richard Barley. He wears armour of 15th century design. The tomb would once have been brightly painted and a few fragments of colour can be seen on the dog at the effigy's feet. The effigy has suffered vandalism at some time - the sword is missing and the hands are damaged. There are some graceful carvings around the tomb, of angels holding shields.

The remains of what was probably a preaching cross

The simple octagonal font

The chancel

This is the finest and main part of the church. It was built between 1260 and 1405. The huge east window dominates the whole church.

It would once have been full of glass and with more decorative tracery, but the window, masonry and the roof fell into ruin after the Dissolution of the Monasteries and some work was lost.

Some fragments of the original 14th century glass can be seen re-used in windows in the chancel.

The reredos with some of the fine glass behind it

The armour wearing effigy and (above) the sedilia

56

Saints and angels

One of the carvings from the reredos

Skull from the brass on the North wall

An angel from the effigy tomb

The choir stalls have some lovely wooden carvings, with the oldest dating from the 15th century.

They include a gryphon and a winged monkey.

The ornate seat on the right of the chancel near the altar, is called a sedilia. It dates from the 14th century and the three seats were made for the Priest, Deacon and sub-deacon to sit during mass.

The altar and the carved panel behind it, which is called a reredos, were made by a local craftsman in 1907. The four figures are probably St John the Baptist, St Peter (with keys), St John and St Mark.

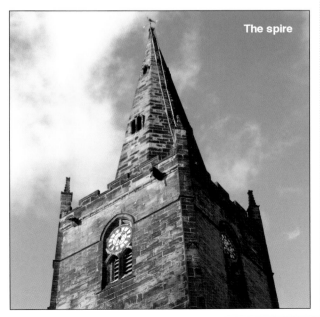

The spire

Fine brasses

The church holds some fine brass monuments. One, The Gomfrey Brass, is in the floor of the chancel, near the rails. It is for Gomfrey brothers Thomas, who was a rector and Richard, who was a Chantry priest. Between the two figures is the shape of a horn, which was once inlaid with brass too. This was to show that the brothers held land under 'cornage' tenure. This meant that they carried out the service of blowing a horn to warn of an enemy approaching.

There are other fine brasses. One to the Fanshawe family is on the North wall of the chancel and below this is another which has characterful skulls drawn on it.

The Fanshawe Brass (right) is made up of eight plates. The largest two show John Fanshawe, (who died in 1578) and his wife Margaret,(who died in 1573). The shields above how the dragon crest of the Fanshawe family (left), the leg in armour of the Eyre family (right) and and a family combined crest in the middle. Below are depicted six children.

■ To find out more about the church visit www.dwhparish. org.uk. There is a good guide book on sale inside the church

Looking towards Millthorpe from Holmesfield

Edward Carpenter

Carpenter's cottage at Millthorpe with George near the door and Carpenter sitting (right)

Millthorpe, a pretty and peaceful village near Holmesfield, may not strike people as a place where fiery ideas were mooted, where Socialists and writers met and discussed ideas of radical politics or illegal sexuality. But at the home of one time resident Edward Carpenter (1844-1929), these were regular events and a procession of famous literary names made their way to his door.

A Bohemian lifestyle

Carpenter was a poet and a mystic. Ideas expressed in his writings were well ahead of his time, and included supporting the rights of women to independence and having a child without being tied to a man. He lived with his male lover and soulmate, George Merrill, at a time when homosexuality was still illegal and the trial of Oscar Wilde was in full debate.

Early years

Edward Carpenter was born in Brighton on August 29, 1844 at 25 Brunswick Square. At 10 he went to Brighton College, later returning home where he lived with parents and sisters. Even in early years he was sad at the lack of life women had, saying his sisters "had absolutely nothing to do except dabble in paints and music and wander aimlessly from room to room to see if anything was going on."

After Brighton College, Edward went to Trinity Hall, Cambridge, winning a prize in 1866 for an essay on modern civilisation. This essay showed his interest in Utopian ideas, harmony and the plight of class struggle. He dreamed of education being provided for all classes of people.

An eccentric academic once wandered Millthorpe and Bradway, raising eyebrows with his bare feet and sandals, bohemian lifestyle and aesthetic ideas...

In May 1869 he became a deacon at the college, and expanded his love of music and writing, producing various books. His love of poetry led him to discover the work of American poet Walt Whitman.

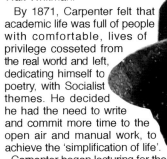

By 1871, Carpenter felt that academic life was full of people with comfortable, lives of privilege cosseted from the real world and left, dedicating himself to poetry, with Socialist themes. He decided he had the need to write and commit more time to the open air and manual work, to achieve the 'simplification of life'.

Carpenter began lecturing for the workers in the autumn of 1873. He taught Astronomy in Leeds, Halifax and Skipton, having a break back to Brighton in 1876 before more lectures in Nottingham and Barnsley.

In April 1877 he went to New Jersey to meet Walt Whitman and was inspired by their similar dreams of education. peace and good living standards and jobs for all.

Socialism and a new home

Carpenter later moved to Sheffield, where he said he felt at ease with the unpretentious people. He lived at the top of Glossop Road, in rooms that he describes in his autobiography My Days and Dreams as **'my lodging place where people were most doleful"**

The Sheffield Socialists

"I heard the world-old cry of the down-trodden and outcast: I saw them advancing always to victory..."

After Long Ages, Toward's Democracy.

Perhaps it was because Carpenter lived in South Yorkshire and Derbyshire, with more radical, working traditions than his birthplace, that he managed to sustain his beliefs and politics more than he would have in London and Cambridge. Forming a Socialist group in Sheffield merely strengthened the interest there already. There were meetings, excursions, public speaking and a favourite haunt of the Socialists was the Wentworth coffee lounge and temperance hotel, at no 19 Holly Street, around where the City Hall is now.

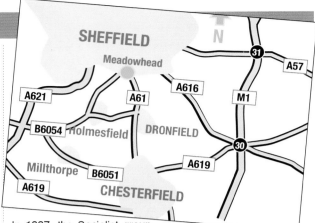

Open air meetings began in 1886, at the corner of Surrey Street and Fargate, sometimes to hundreds of people.

PHOTO: SHEFFIELD NEWSPAPERS ARCHIVES

> The meeting place 'monolith' on the corner of Surrey Street and Fargate

In 1887, the Socialist group found a place to have as a meeting centre, at Scotland Street, in Sheffield city centre. It had been an old debtor's jail and was called the Commonwealth Cafe. Carpenter lived in an attic at the top of the building for a year or so, above much of the city noise:

"In the early morning at 5am there was the strident sound of the hammers and the clattering of innumerable clogs of men and girls going to their work and on till late at night there were drunken cries and shouting.
Far around stretched nothing but factory chimneys and foul courts inhabited by the wretched workers."

There were indeed an amazing number and variety of 'wretched workers' in the courts at the old debtor's jail.

Here are a few examples, from he street directory of 1884:

Court 13: Alfred Loe, Clock cleaner

Court 9, No.69½: Benjamin Coldwell, brass finisher

Court 22, No.127½: Thomas Howson, corkscrew manufacturer

No. 135: John Deakin Ivory Cutter, as well as various others including a hatter, fishmonger, tailor, milk seller, and second hand clothes shops.

Edward Carpenter must have been a strange addition to this collection of humanity, He spent his spare time there playing his harmonium and compiling Chants of labour – A Song Book of the People.

Many meetings with the unemployed were held at the cafe, which held 150 and was often overflowing. One open air demonstration at West Bar overflowed into Paradise Square.

Obtaining Paradise

In 1879 one of Carpenter's students, a scythemaker called Albert Fearnehough, invited him to visit his cottage and farm at Bradway, near Sheffield, on land owned by a man with Socialist beliefs, called Charles Fox, Albert lived there with his wife and two children. Carpenter loved it all and moved in there. He wanted to achieve his aims of 'the simplification of life.'

In 1880, Carpenter's mother died, and his father soon after in 1882, leaving some inheritance, which Carpenter used to buy a smallholding at Millthorpe, near Holmesfield. He built a house on 7 acres of land. The Fearnehough's came too, to help share the housekeeping and gardening.

COVER AND PAGE FROM CARPENTER'S CHANTS OF LABOUR SONG BOOK

Millthorpe

Edward Carpenter's old home at Millthorpe and the view

Edward Carpenter: homosexual, revolutionary, founder of a farming commune

The socialist who shocked Victorian Sheffield

THIS is the story of a revolutionary who shocked Sheffield by his lifestyle around the turn of the century. He was a homosexual who openly lived with his lovers at a commune farm – a believer in sexual as well as social revolution. At the height of his fame, thousands of Sheffield people would listen to his speeches and his books were read all over the world. The man is brought back to life in a new book by Sheila Rowbotham," STEVE CHILDS reports.

An article about Carpenter and some of his sandals

The nearest railway station was four miles away and visitors and admirers had to walk to the cottage. Here they became market gardeners, taking produce for sale in Sheffield and Chesterfield on a cart.

At one end of his cottage, Carpenter had a small workshop, where he made sandals for himself and his friends. He wore sandals all the time, (probably inspired by his visits abroad), and this added to his eccentric reputation, as well as his wide brimmed felt hats, loose shirts, knicker bocker type tweed suits and long stockings.

Carpenter built a little summer house by the brook in the garden, where he did much of his writing. He used the nearby barn to put on plays, including St George and the Dragon in 1913. He also led whit sings at the local cricket club field.

The Fearnehough's left in 1893, but others took their place. One of Carpenter's closest friends was George Hukin, a razor grinder from Bath Street. He and his wife Fannie later moved to a cottage near Holmesfield to join Carpenter.

The place at Millthorpe soon became a magnet for the free thinkers and eccentrics who had heard of Carpener and felt a kinship with him:

"faddists of all sorts and kinds considered me their special prey. I don't know what I had done to deserve this - but so it was. Vegetarians, dress reformers, temperance orators, spiritualists, secularists, anti- vivisectionists, socialists, anarchists - and others of very serious mien and character - would call and insist in the most determined way on my joining their crusades - so that some-times I had almost to barricade myself against them.
A friend suggested (and the idea was not a bad one) that I should put up at the gate a board bearing the legend "To the Asylum" on it.
Then the real lunatics would probably avoid the neighbourhood."

My Days and Dreams - 'Millthorpia'

Later Carpenter shared his home with a younger man called George Merrill. He had met Merrill in 1891, in a railway carriage from Sheffield to Totley. Merrill was from a hard background, with an unemployed father with a drink problem. Carpenter helped him get a job at The Sheffield Telegraph, as a cleaner, by providing a reference. With his wages he ran a little cottage in a poor part of Sheffield, at 79 Edward Street, where he lived with his mother. Carpenter made George a pair of sandals, which earned him some odd looks from his neighbours.

He moved in with Carpenter and they were very happy together. Carpenter said George made house- work "an artistic pleasure". Many of the locals were dubious of the relationship. Homosexuality was still illegal then, and the Oscar Wilde trial of 1895 was in flow. Two men living together with no woman to look after them was seen as odd. Many thought George was just Edward's servant.

It was a testimony to Carpenter's personality and likeability that any scandal was minimal, though there were letters of protest to the Sheffield Telegraph in 1908, from an Irishman called O'Brien.

In 1922 Edward and George left Sheffield for Guildford. In 1928 George died and Edward died just a year later. They are buried together in the Mount Cemetery, Guildford.

Dore and Totley railway station, about the time that Carpenter met George Merrill

A Literary Legacy

Literary success

The influence of Carpenter's writings on Socialism, idealism and sexuality were at a height just before the First World War. His books have been translated into many languages.

Carpenter in his trademark sandals

His most well known works are probably the epic poem cycle 'Toward's Democracy' and his autobiography, My Days and Dreams. Other works include The Intermediate Sex and Love's Coming of Age.

Many literary figures visited the community at Millthorpe, including W.B Yeats, E.M. Forster, Bernard Shaw and H.G. Wells.

E.M. Forster wrote his novel Maurice after being inspired by a visit there in 1913 and the way Carpenter and his friends expressed their homosexual feelings. Forster said of Carpenter,

"He wasn't happy in the class in which he was born. He didn't revolt from a sense of duty, or to make a splash, but because he wanted to.

In his "Terminal Note" to Maurice Forster tells how the novel Maurice came to be written:

It was the direct result of a visit to Edward Carpenter at Millthorpe. Carpenter . . . was a socialist who ignored industrialism and a simple-lifer with an independent income and a . . . believer in the love of comrades, whom he sometimes called Uranians. It was this last aspect of him that attracted me in my loneliness. . . . I approached him . . . as one approaches a savior. It must have been on my second or third visit to the shrine that the spark was kindled as he and his comrade George Merrill combined to make a profound impression on me and to touch a creative spring."

Forster and Carpenter also shared a fascination with India. Carpenter had visited there in 1890, meditating with religious teachers, which was adventurous travelling for the era.

Nowadays his works are not widely known, but well worth reading to rediscover the essays and poems. This man with ideas and a lifestyle that defied the conventions of the time he was born into had an influence on many famous names of the literary and political world.

■ **Most of Edward Carpenters letters and writings are held in the Carpenter Collection at Sheffield Archives, 52 Shoreham Street, Sheffield, Sheffield S1 4SP Telephone: (0114) 203 9395**

■ **Carpenter's cottage, on Cordwell Lane, is now Carpenter House Bed and Breakfast accommodation.**

PHOTOS: THE STAR ARCHIVES

Carpenter's 'Local'

The Royal Oak in Millthorpe is just down the road from Carpenter's old cottage. This quaint establishment is over 300 years old and used to be a an old mill. It was enlarged and turned into a public house in 1840.

Edward Carpenter was a frequent visitor and used to play the piano in the front room there.

Nowadays it is a popuar place for a meal or drink and has a nice beer garden.

■ The Royal Oak: 0114 2890870

A friend's resting place

Edward Carpenter's close friend George Hukin and his wife Fanny are buried in Holmesfield church. Carpenter had said of him in his autobiogrphy:

"George E Hukin, with his Dutch featured face and Dutch build - no speaker in public - but though young an excellent help at our committee meetings, where his shrewd, strong brain and tactful nature gave his counsels much weight, and always from the beginning an ally of mine."

Holmesfield church and (above) George Hukin's grave

Around Holmesfield

Above, ford at Millthorpe. Below, leafy lane at Millthorpe

Marsh marigolds at Unthank

Walking towards Millthorpe on an old packhorse track

View across fields from from Unthank

Fanshawe Gate Hall, which dates back to the 13th century

Fanshawe Gate Hall

A picturesque old hall
with a wonderful
garden...

The old hall in the picture book garden

Just past the village of Holmesfield, as you travel from Sheffield towards Owler Bar, is a turning off to the right which leads down to this timeless and lovely old family home.

Origins

Fanshawe Gate Hall was owned by the Fanshawe Family from 1260 until 1944. The people who live there now, John and Cynthia Ramsden, have been there since 1959, and are only the fourth owners in over 700 years. They have spent much time and love restoring the house and gardens and it is a wonderful home full of character.

Although Fanshawe Gate Hall dates back to the 13th century, the architecture of the present house is predominantly 16th century. It was once much larger, but was reduced in size in 1634. There is a tithe barn and this is now being restored, along with the rest of the property .Over the past decade or so, the garden has been substantially redesigned in the style of the Tudor era, as this was the century when the Fanshawe family was at the height of its influence.

The wrought iron gates, with the Fanshawe coat of arms

[Map showing roads: To Sheffield, A625, A57, A621, A6102, Fanshawe Gate Hall, Owler Bar, A6102, DRONFIELD, N, B6054, HOLMESFIELD, B6051, A61]

The Fanshawe Family

Henry Fanshawe is one of the more famous members of the family. He became 'Remembrancer of the Exchequer' to Queen Elizabeth 1st in 1566. He was the first of nine members of the Fanshawe family to hold this post.

The name of Henry Fanshawe is also remembered in the name of a school in Dronfield, which was founded under his will.

One of the better documented members of the family is Lady Ann Fanshawe. She married her second cousin Richard Fanshawe in 1644, during the English Civil War. He was an official in the court of King Charles 1st.

Ann wrote memoirs in her later life, to give to her only surviving son and these provide a first hand account of the war and the imprisonment and execution of King Charles.

She also tells of how her mother was born at Fanshawe Gate Hall, the youngest daughter of Robert Fanshawe, who had the grand total of 12 sons and two daughters. (The Ramsden family consists of a more modest five children!)

The Fanshawe coat of arms has been incorporated into the wind vane and the wrought iron entrance gates.

The Garden

The Dovecote

There is a lovely old 16th century dovecote in the garden, which was restored by one of the Ramsden's sons and a neighbour. It is made of the same Derbyshire sandstone as the 16th century hall.

The dovecote has won an award from the Council for the Protection of Rural England. It is now home once again to doves, beautiful white ones that can be seen sitting there or on the other rooves, adding grace to the garden.

The old dovecote (right) and waterfall (left)

The same stone is seen in the retaining walls of the courtyard and in the walled garden. The other boundaries are traditional Derbyshire drystone walls.

The ties with the farming past can be seen in the mushroom-shaped staddle stones. These would have been used to support corn before threshing to stop it getting wet or eaten by rats. Now they make interesting features hidden in the undergrowth.

There are also several millstones to be found discarded in the garden. These are now made into features, planted with hostas and alpines.

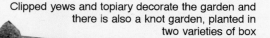

Clipped yews and topiary decorate the garden and there is also a knot garden, planted in two varieties of box

The waterfall

The Ramsden's son constructed the waterfall in the courtyard.

This has lovely stonework in the form of terraced shelves and also a lions head water spout. The water cascades down from the orchard to the courtyard into a plant filled pool.

The plants

Many of the plants have been chosen because they would have been well known 400 years ago and could well have been part of the original planting.

The east facing borders on either side of the entrance to the house contain Aconitum, Digitalis, Alcea rosea, Achillea, Malva, Lychnis, Dianthus, Artemisia, Origanum, Salvia, Lathyrus.

The upper walled garden has herbaceous, variegated and fern planting, terracing and lawns.

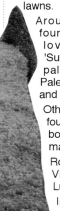

A characterful old door at the hall

Around the lion head fountain are moisture loving plants, including Sambucus racemosa 'Sutherland Gold', Cornus alba Spaethii', Iris ensata, Iris pallida 'Variegata', Persicaria virginiana 'Painter's Palette', Rodgersia pinnata. 'Elegans', Primula bulleyana and hostas.

Other plants complement the period of the house, often found in a traditional cottage garden. The south facing borders in front of the house and the borders of the main lawn include:

Rosa species, Lythrum, Lilium, Peaonia, Delphinium, Viola, Papaver, Phlox, Geranium, Campanula, Lupinus, Lunaria, Eryngium, Filipendula and Geum

In the walled "Elizabethan" garden is a 'nuttery'. A different variety of nut tree is, or will be, planted for each of the Ramsden's grandchildren.

A lifelong project

Ongoing work

The old orchard at Fanshawe Gate Hall is under restoration, and the new design features a natural wildlife pond and a terraced landscape based upon a medieval tiltyard layout. The trees are local, old varieties of fruit. The old 'bowl' shape of the pond is reputed to be part of an old moat for the hall and so is very appropriate.

Many ponds and wetland have disappeared in the countryside due to land reclamation and agriculture and the pond will be a valuable wildlife resource.

Water is supplied to the pond in two ways. One way is from a gravity fed 800 gallon storage tank in the field opposite the entrance of the hall. The other way is for dry periods, when a pumped supply boosts the water feed. The water is pumped from an old 65 ft deep well, via a trough and a culvert and so into the pond as a stream.

Plants in or near the pond include Water Crowfoot, Water Violet, Bog Bean, kingcup and Flag Iris as well as Monkshood, Yarrow, Angelica, Meadowsweet and Purple Loosestrife.

Pond and Water Crowfoot

A welcoming and quirky summerhouse in the garden. This dates from about 1901 and once had a thatched roof

Roses climb over the old stonework of the hall

Visiting Fanshawe Gate Hall

Open Days

Open days at Fanshawe Gate Hall are one of the the highlights of the garden viewing year for many visitors.

The garden is open several times during the year and well worth a visit. There is a small entrance fee. Any money made is given to local charities or projects. There are refreshments usually available at the open days, with tea, coffee, cream teas and delicious cakes and Ploughman's lunches to tempt.

There is also a plant stall selling plants raised from their own cuttings and seeds.

Feathered occupants of the stable block

Below: Decoration on the gate post

Above: The loft and stables. Top: The walled garden

To find out when the garden is open, look in the local press or look out for leaflets. Alternatively, look at the hall's website at **www.fgh.org.uk**

To get to Fanshawe Gate Hall, follow the B6054 leaving the village of Holmesfield heading towards Owler Bar. Take the first right turn after the Robin Hood Pub. Go down the lane and, for parking, turn left into the old stackyard 100 yards after the main entrance.

The garden is usually open from 11am to 5pm.

A book about the garden

A personal account of how the garden at Fanshawe Gate Hall has been developed over the last decades was written by Cynthia Ramsden. Entitled "A Garden in my Life", it raised more than £8,000 for two cancer charities.

At the time of writing, the book has sold out, but more may be printed in the future.

Cynthia Ramsden's book about the hall and it's garden

The orchard at Fanshawe Gate Hall

PHOTOGRAPH: Mark Ramsden

A view from Fanshawe Gate Hall towards Totley

Bluebells

One of the most magical sights to be seen in woodland is a carpet of bluebells, their blue haze set amid the vivid green of spring grass

A magical bluebell wood - a place of enchantment?

Bluebells are a flower that seem to often be associated with fairies and nursery rhymes. A bluebell wood, with the lovely flowers dappled in sunlight through leaves, has an almost otherworldly quality and it is not hard to see why they are seen as magical places.

Fairy led

In and out the dusky bluebells,
in and out the dusky bluebells,
in and out the dusky bluebells
I'll be your leader.
Rat-a-tat-a-tat-ter on her shoulder...

Many children know this cheerful little song about dusky bluebells, sung as they in turn make arches and dance underneath in a musical game. But it can also be seen as a rather eerie warning not to wander into a magical bluebell wood.

The bells of the flowers were said to ring and summon the fairies to their gatherings in the woods.

Enter there and perhaps you could be put under a spell by the sweet and heady scent of the blooms, like Dorothy in the Wizard of Oz when the pollen from the beanfield puts her to sleep.

Or maybe you could be tapped on the shoulder and led away to enchantment, a prisoner in fairyland.

Another rhyme, 'Blue and green should never be seen except on an Irish fairy queen' could well be refering to the colous of the bluebell wood - for fairies alone and not for the humanchild.

With all this folklore woven into our lives and with the beauty of the plant, it has become an iconic favourite.

Under threat

Now this favourite plant of British broadleaved woodlands is threatened. As well as loss of habitat by more building, and more woods being turned over to farming, over zealous collection of the bulbs has been a problem. Since 1998 it has been illegal for anyone to collect native bluebells from the wild for sale. This is to stop people digging bulbs up and selling them to garden centres.

Overfriendly invader

The biggest threat however is from another species of bluebell. The Spanish bluebell, introduced as an ornamental garden plant. It is causing hybridisation and creating a mixture of itself and the native bluebell.

To try and halt this risk to our native plant, people are being encouraged not to plant the Spanish variety, or at least not near any native bluebells or in the wild. If you buy bluebells from a garden centre make sure they are the native varety, collected legally from a sustainable source.

In March 2003 a 'Bluebells for Britain' survey was carried out and thousands of people recorded the different species they saw. The survey was by Plantlife International (www.plantlife,org.uk) and gave useful information about how widespread the hybrids are. Not surprisingly the more built up areas had more Spanish or hybrid types, due to them being planted in gardens and native ones were most often recorded in broadleaved woodland.

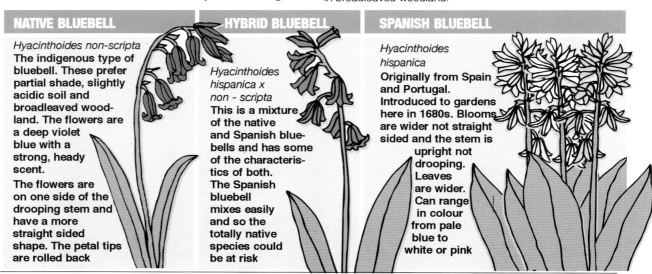

NATIVE BLUEBELL	HYBRID BLUEBELL	SPANISH BLUEBELL
Hyacinthoides non-scripta **The indigenous type of bluebell. These prefer partial shade, slightly acidic soil and broadleaved woodland. The flowers are a deep violet blue with a strong, heady scent.** **The flowers are on one side of the drooping stem and have a more straight sided shape. The petal tips are rolled back**	*Hyacinthoides hispanica x non - scripta* **This is a mixture of the native and Spanish bluebells and has some of the characteristics of both. The Spanish bluebell mixes easily and so the totally native species could be at risk**	*Hyacinthoides hispanica* **Originally from Spain and Portugal. Introduced to gardens here in 1680s. Blooms are wider not straight sided and the stem is upright not drooping. Leaves are wider. Can range in colour from pale blue to white or pink**

Pentrich revolution

Pentrich, between Alftreton and Ripley was the setting for a short lived revolution on June 9th, 1817

Rebel leader Jeremiah Brandreth, based on a drawing made during his trial

Pentrich, just north of Ripley, was the site of England's last revolution, which was a disastrously unorganised affair resulting in execution for some of the rebels and deportation or jail for others.

Hardship and unrest

After the battle of Waterloo in 1815, there was unrest in the country due to the high price of food and general standard of living for the common man. There had been a slump in work due to people cutting back and so many people were unemployed during the resulting recession. The iron and textile industries in and around Pentrich were hit hard.

Those who did have work were paid low wages and so found it hard to make ends meet.

As if that was not bad enough the harvest of 1816 had been poor due to bad weather. Food got more scare and prices went up even more.

By 1817 people felt that the Government was totally unrepresentative of the them and their problems. The monarchy too, was angering its subjects. The Prince Regent was enjoying an extravagant lifestyle whilst the common people were finding it hard to afford to live and suffering hardships.

People were restless for improvement and change. Groups eager for political reform began to form and meet.

The government noticed these seeds of unrest and forbade groups of 50 or more to gather. The memory of the French Revolution was still fresh and they didn't want the same thing to develop on their own doorstep.

One of the people who was active in these reform meetings was a man called Thomas Bacon, a framework knitter who lived in Pentrich. He went to various meetings around the area and brought back stories to his local meetings of a plan to met with many others from the North and Midlands and march to London, to overthrow the government.

What he and the others at these meetings didn't know was that a man named Oliver, a newcomer to the area, was in fact a government spy.

Oliver attended meetings and eventually was even encouraging people to take part in the rally and march. He also fed back any information and plans he heard and the Government responded by breaking up meetings and arresting ringleaders.

Thomas Bacon had a warrant out for his arrest and went into hiding. When the march did happen he was not a participant.

The leadership of the group was passed from Bacon to a man named Jeremiah Brandreth. He was an unemployed frame knitter. He came to Pentrich on June 5th 1817. Attending the meetings in a barn and public houses he told the people that the march was planned for June 9th, setting off from Nottingham at 10pm. On the way they would be joined by others and then carry on to London. Arms would be collected as they went along. They had pikes, scythes and a few guns.

March and capture

The 10pm meeting time came. Men walked through the rainy darkness to assemble at a barn in South Wingfield. They knocked on doors as they went, attempting to force the menfolk within to join them. Not all were sympathetic to the cause and so tried to hide or resist.

At one house a widow refused to give the night callers any weapons and a scuffle broke out. Her servant Robert Walters was shot and killed, the only fatality that night.

Now it was even more serious and the men were more determined. They carried on to Butterley Ironworks, where Brandreth demanded arms and some shot for cannons. They did not get any.

A little less optimistic, many of the marchers decided to abandon the fledgling revolution and go home. The others carried on to get as far as the Nottinghamshire border. Here they met with soldiers, the King's Hussars. There was a skirmish and arrests. Some people managed to escape, disappearing into the darkness and hiding in bushes and outbuildings until it was clear.

CHESTERFIELD
To Chapel-en-le-Frith
A61
A619
Clay cross
A61
A617
Alfreton
Pentrich
A38
To Mansfield
Belper
Ripley
To Derby

Revolution aftermath

After a short trial, the rebel leader Jeremiah Brandreth and two other ringleaders, Isaac Ludlam and William Turner, were hanged. They were also beheaded. Six more were jailed and fourteen others were transported to a penal colony in Australia.

The journey to Australia was a punishment in itself, with harsh conditions and scurvy, It was a long and hard ordeal.

The transported men were eventually given full pardons. It is thought that none of them ever came back to Pentrich.

The poet Shelley wrote a lament after the hangings "An address &c." which is also known as "We pity the plumage but forget the dying bird."

This was written because the Prince Regent's daughter - one of the 'plumage' Royals, had died in childbirth at the time of the hangings and she was getting more public sympathy than the less wealthy but just as human hanged men.

Punishment for the village

Pentrich suffered for the rebel's impertinence. Houses of those involved in the revolutionary march were pulled down, and their lands given to others. Some people in the village turned informer, shopping the ones who had escaped the Hussars or who had been involved, or they suspected of being involved. The informers who gave evidence were sometimes given the accused's land as reward.

The village, once more important than nearby Ripley, was a broken place. It had once belonged to Darley Abbey, until 1634, when it became part of the Chatsworth estate and owned by the Duke of Devonshire.

The Butterley Ironworks were esteemed and one of their later contracts included the structure of St Pancras Station, London. It was one of the work sources in Pentrich, along with a colliery, the textile industry and faming. The occupations of the captured revolutionaries, listed below, reflect this.

Two of the plaques that mark the route and important sites of the Pentrich Revolution, the place where Thomas Bacon hid and the barn where the rebels met to plan the march

Below left, a list of the rebels and their fates

Hanged

JEREMIAH BRANDRETH, 31, Frame work knitter. from Sutton-in-Ashfield

ISAAC LUDLAM, 52, Stone-getter from South Wingfield
WILLIAM TURNER, 46, Stonemason from South Wingfield

Transported

THOMAS BACON, 64, Frame work knitter. from Pentrich
JOHN BACON, 54, Frame work knitter. from Pentrich
GEORGE BRASSINGTON, 33, Miner from Pentrich
GERMAN BUXTON, 31, Miner from Alfreton
JOHN HILL, 29, Frame work knitter. from South Wingfield
SAMUEL HUNT, 24, Farmer from South Wingfield
JOHN MCKESSWICK, 38, Frame work knitter from Heanor
JOHN ONION, 49, Iron Worker from Pentrich
EDWARD TURNER, 34, Stonemason from South Wingfield
JOSEPH TURNER, 18, Clerk from South Wingfield
GEORGE WEIGHTMAN, 26, Sawyer from Pentrich
THOMAS BETTISON, 33, Miner from Alfreton
JOSIAH GODBER, 54, Labourer from Pentrich
JOSEPH RAWSON, 31, Frame work knitter from Alfreton

Jailed

JOHN MOORE, 49, Frame work knitter from Pentrich
EDWARD MOORE, 27, Shoemaker from Pentrich
WILLIAM WEIGHTMAN, 27, Labourer from Pentrich
WILLIAM HARDWICK, 24, Collier from Pentrich
ALEXANDER JOHNSON, 24, Labourer from Pentrich
CHARLES SWAINE, 33, Frame work knitter. from South Wingfield

Pentrich remembers

The fact that the village of Pentrich suffered in 1817 and was as a result overtaken in growth and importance by Ripley, means that the rural character of the place has been kept quite well.

However not many traces or evidence remain from the time of the revolution and the village looked very different then. The church of St. Matthew is one of the few buildings that was there in 1817 to bear witness to the events.

In the village there are plaques to mark the revolution trail and highlight important places and buildings..

The story of the revolution is well told by the Pentrich Historical Society on a website at **www.pentrich.org.uk** with details of the village trail.

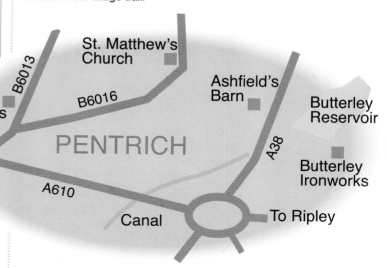

Cromford Canal

A once bustling wharf and canal is now a haven for wildlife and a popular trail for walkers, with fascinating historic sites along the way

PICTURE: Courtesy of Friends of the Cromford Canal

An old photograph of Cromford Wharf. Willersley Castle can just be made out above the cabin of the boat Shamrock, belonging to W Dawes & Sons of Cromford. Then there is the existing 'Gothic' warehouse (with castellated face towards Willersely Castle). The castellations were to make it more acttractive and so give less of an impression of industry in the view from the castle. To the right is the existing wharfinger's house and above it Cromford Church. Today you cannot see the church from here because of the tree growth. The inset shows the warehouse today.

Just over the road from Cromford Mill is the wharf for Cromford canal, built in the 18th century as a transport route for local businesses.

Beginnings

The Cromford Canal was fully open by August 1794, but the beginnings were a few years before that, when a meeting in Matlock proposed a canal to link the southern side of the Peak District to the Erewash Canal and so develop the export of the limestone being quarried and burnt in the area. Also the import of coal, household goods etc. Pack horses were being used, but were slow and costly and a more efficient way to move products was needed.

Sir Richard Arkwright was invited to be a figurehead for the canal project and help see it through Parliament, though he did not always agree with the way it was handled. One major issue involved the location of the Wharf, which was eventually built on what had been the garden of his home, Rock House. Sadly Arkwright died in 1792 and so did not see the completion of the canal in his lifetime.

The canal, built by William Jessop and Benjamin Outram, and now a serene place to walk, was once busy with boats.

In the photograph above, it is coal which is being transported. The last use of Cromford Wharf was as a coal wharf. The coal can be seen stacked in a pile after being taken from the boat, ready to be taken by the waiting horses and carts and distributed.

Further along the canal, an aqueduct, (1793) designed by William Jessop, takes the canal over the River Derwent.

In 1802 a privately owned branch of the canal, the Lea Wood or Nightingale Branch, built by Peter Nightingale, was opened.

Peter Nightingale later left his estate to the father of Florence Nightingale, the famous Lady of The Lamp. This new branch provided access to a number of quarries, a lead-works, a cotton mill and a hat factory.

Walking along the Lea arm of the canal will bring you to the John Smedley Mills at Lea Bridge. The Smedley mill was once a cotton mill, founded in 1784, by Peter Nightingale.

The mill are still making textiles and famous Smedley sweaters today.

A view from the wharf warehouse

You will see ducks and perhaps a water vole too

Ducks paddle along the canal

Above is the bridge at Smedley Mills

High Peak Junction

High Peak Junction is about a 30 minute walk from the wharf. Here there are early railway buildings and a small museum.

The junction is where the canal joined up with the Cromford and High Peak Railway. This unique railway opened in 1831 and was one of the earliest in Britain. It linked the Cromford Canal with the Peak Forest Canal, at Whaley Bridge.

Originally on the railway, horses pulled wagons on the straight stretches and steam powered beam engines were used to pull the wagons up inclines.

"Who would have thought of a railway over such acclivities and apparently inaccessible tracts."
From The Gem of the Peak, Adam, 1851

High Peak Junction, with restored workshops

Pumps and engines

A little further along the canal from High Peak Junction is the 1849 Leawood Pumphouse. It has a tall, 29m high chimney. Open days are held here to see the steam powered beam engine at work. This engine pumps water from the River Derwent into the canal, at about 31 tons per minute.

Also on one of the inclines along the old railway route near the canal is the Middleton Top Winding Engine, built in 1829 to raise and lower wagons on the incline. It is the only survivor of the eight which once stood along the line. The engine, run originally on steam, now uses air from a compressor when it is in operation on demonstration days. There is a visitor centre and cycle hire at the site.

Black Rock

Overlooking the High Peak Trail at the top of Cromford Hill, these rocks are popular with climbers and families. There are good views and forest trails.

End of an era

As railways and roads became more widely used, the canal system began to decline. In 1936 the Lea Wood Branch of the Cromford Canal was closed and the canal was later abandoned, becoming weeded over and hidden by undergrowth. The last train crossed the Peak District on the Cromford and High Peak Railway in 1967, and the old line is now the High Peak Trail, almost 18 miles long.

The High Peak Junction Workshops (1830) have been restored and house an Information and Exhibition Centre.

New beginnings

Following the closure of The Cromford and High Peak Railway, the land was purchased jointly by Derbyshire County Council and the Peak Park Planning Board, in partnership with the Countryside Commission and was converted into the High Peak Trail.

The Friends of the Cromford Canal was formed in 2002 with the aim of restoring this historic canal to navigation throughout its length.

The Friends of Cromford Canal:
■ www.cromfordcanal.org.uk ■ Telephone: 0115 946 4479

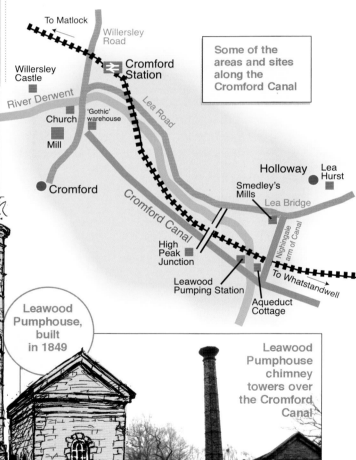

Some of the areas and sites along the Cromford Canal

To Matlock
Willersley Road
Willersley Castle
Cromford Station
River Derwent
Church
'Gothic' warehouse
Mill
Lea Road
Cromford
Holloway
Lea Hurst
Smedley's Mills
Lea Bridge
Cromford Canal
High Peak Junction
Nightingale arm of Canal
Leawood Pumping Station
Aqueduct Cottage
To Whatstandwell

Leawood Pumphouse, built in 1849

Leawood Pumphouse chimney towers over the Cromford Canal

Aqueduct Cottage

PICTURE: Courtesy of Friends of the Cromford Canal

This picturesque cottage was built by Peter Nightingale, probably for the keeper of the lock at the Leawood Arm of the Cromford Canal to live in. It was known as Aqueduct Cottage. There were strict rules about maintaining the correct water levels in the canal and access for boats, so a lock keeper was needed to ensure this.

Today the cottage presents a very different picture as the years have taken their toll and it is now a ruin.

Leawood Pump House

Cromford Mills

Remains of the second mill are in the foreground

Richard Arkwright's Cromford Mills are part of the Derwent Valley Mills, a World Heritage Site

The cotton mills of the Derwent Valley are recognised as the birthplace of the factory system, where revolutionary machinery designed by Sir Richard Arkwright increased the production and output of the cotton industry.

A valued product

Cotton was one of the country's imports by the 18th century. The merchants who imported the raw cotton gave it out to workers for manufacture. Whole families were involved in the work, which was cleaning, carding, spinning and weaving. The men and older boys did the weaving. Weaver's cottages had large, wide windows to allow more light into the rooms.

When the cloth was finished, the merchants collected it and paid for the work done. It was a time consuming process with many hours labour costs. A way of making the yarn faster was needed to keep up with the growing demand. It was a man named Richard Arkwright who eventually helped revolutionise the industry.

Richard Arkwright (1732-1792)

Born in Preston, the son of a tailor, Arkwright grew up in a large, poor family, with 12 siblings. He didn't get much schooling and later became a barber and wig maker. He travelled around the country selling wigs and so met people involved in the cotton trade. Talking to these traders, Arkwright realised that if he could make efficient machinery to help produce more cotton, it would make him a fortune.

He made models of machinery and when he teamed up with a clockmaker called John Kay, in 1768, they came up with the design for a roller spinning machine. This device later became known as the 'water frame.'

Needing financial backing, the two men joined with two more partners. Mr Jedediah Strutt of Nottingham, a stocking manufacturer, was impressed with the invention and he and his partner Mr Samuel Need went into business with Arkwright. The roller spinning machine was patented and then brought into use at a horse powered mill in Nottingham.

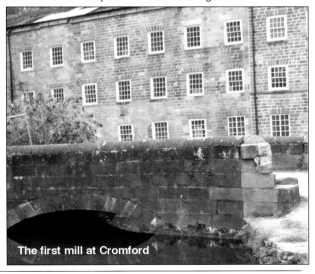

The first mill at Cromford

Around the mill

A new mill and expansions

In 1771, Arkwright built a mill at Cromford. This new mill used water from Cromford Sough (a sough is a drain from a lead mine) and later from Bonsall Brook. Cromford Mill was the world's first successful water powered cotton spinning mill.

A big new mill needed a large workforce. Many workers were found locally, others were encouraged to move to the area and Arkwright and his son, also named Richard, built up a community around the mills. Cottages, a church and a hotel were built, as well as a school so the children working at the mill could learn to read and write.

The first mill at Cromford was built in 1771 and is towards the back of the site as you enter. The site and remains of a second mill of 1776, which burned down in 1890, has a viewing platform over it. From this you can see the water cascading down into the pit where the waterwheel used to be. An annexe to the second mill, straight in front of you when you stand on the viewing platform, was built in1780.

By 1783, the water power at Cromford could not keep up with demand for textile production and so Arkwright expanded production with another mill near Matlock Bath, Masson Mill, with a more powerful water supply. (see the chapter on Masson Mill). Arkwright also built mills at other sites around the country and his new technique was copied throughout the world.

Richard Arkwright became wealthy and famous because of his contributions to the cotton industry, and was knighted in 1787, when he was the High Sheriff of Derby.

Arkwright's 'Castle'

Sir Richard Arkwright lived in a house next to his mill, at Cromford. He also had built a grand new home, Willersley Castle, which stands on a hill above the mill.

In 1792, Arkwright died at the age of 60 without having lived in his castle; a fire had delayed its completition.

Cromford Church, Arkwright's final resting place

At first, Arkwright was buried at St Giles in Matlock, but later his body was moved to the church he had built at Cromford.

His Castle is now a hotel and conference centre.

A new life for old buildings

The Cromford buildings were put to other uses after the cotton mills closed, including a brewery, laundries, cheese warehousing and finally, in 1922, the production of colour pigments for paints and dyes. which used the place until 1979.

Sir Richard Arkwright's Cromford Mills are now at the heart of the Derwent Valley Mills World Heritage Site, which runs from Masson Mill all the way down the valley to Derby..

The Arkwright Society purchased Cromford Mill in 1979 and it is now home to a visitors centre, shops and a cafe.

There is also a large Conference Centre at Cromford Mills, with a variety of meeting and function rooms.

■ **Cromford Conference Centre: 01629 825995**

■ **e mail: visitor services@arkwrightsociety.org.uk**

The mills lie just off the A6 Derby-Matlock road at Cromford. Buses from Matlock pass the gate of the mills.

Regular trains running between Derby and Matlock stop at Cromford Station.

■ **The Arkwright Society has done and still is doing an enormous amount of restoration work at Cromford Mills. Restoration of Cromford Railway Station, the only original station within the Derwent Valley Mills World HeritageSite, is one of the projects. This would provide a portal into the site.**

Their address is: The Arkwright Society, Cromford Mill, Mill Lane, Cromford, Derbyshire DE4 3RQ

■ **Telephone: 01629 823256**

■ **www.arkwrightsociety.org.uk**

■ **www.cromfordmill.co.uk**

Cromford Mill, at the heart of the Derwent Valley mills World Heritage Site

Masson Mills

Sir Richard
Arkwright's
Masson
Mill

The historic Masson Mills at Matlock
Bath was Arkwright's showpiece and
now holds a working Textiles Museum

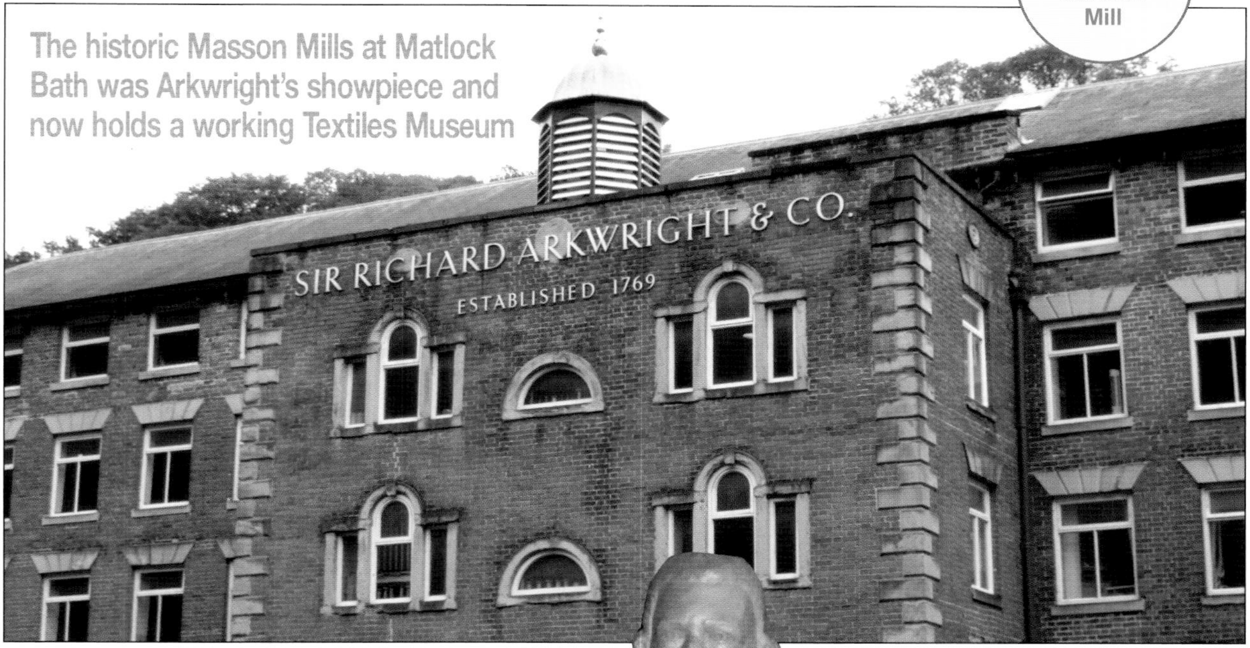

SIR RICHARD ARKWRIGHT & CO.

ESTABLISHED 1769

The impressive mill at Masson was also
built by Richard Arkwright, on the banks of
the River Derwent, in Matlock Bath.

Branching out

A few years after setting up business at
Cromford, Arkwright wanted to expand
his site. Business was booming and
the mills at Cromford could not keep
up with demand, so Arkwright continued

his developments with this new mill. It was sited
to harness the River Derwent, not the sough
and brook as at Cromford, and this produced
much more power.

The mill was built in 1783 and is a
Venetian style, showpiece from
when Arkwright was at the height of
his career. Today the mills are
home to a fascinating museum
of the textile industry, sited in
the oldest, 18th century, original
part of the site.

When visiting, you are given
a ticket, with which you can
'clock in' at the door. Inside,
the place has not changed
since Arkwright's time in some
parts. The stair-
way is original
and inside is
still the old teth-
ering ring where
Arkwright used to
tie his horse if it
was raining.

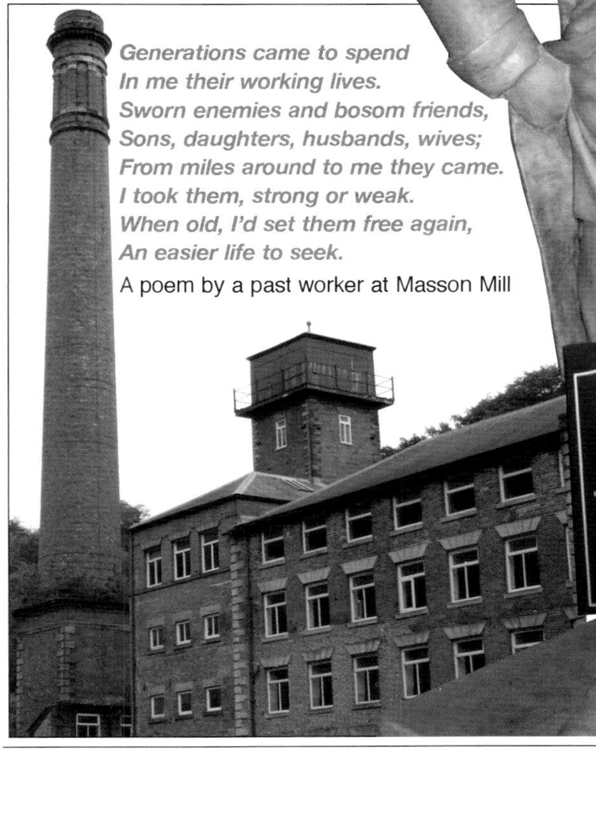

Generations came to spend
In me their working lives.
Sworn enemies and bosom friends,
Sons, daughters, husbands, wives;
From miles around to me they came.
I took them, strong or weak.
When old, I'd set them free again,
An easier life to seek.

A poem by a past worker at Masson Mill

Left:
Statue of
Richard
Arkwright
at Masson
mills.
Right: The
'clocking
in' clock

The threads of industry

PICTURE: By Roger Grayson. By courtesy of the Derbyshire Times and The Chad

A bird's eye view of Masson Mill and the river

Warp speed!

Masson Mill continued to develop, with Arkwright's family and later the English Sewing Cotton Company, to whom the family sold the business, extending the original mill over the years. The impressive chimney dates from 1907.

The historic working machinery in the museum is fascinating and there are shuttles and bobbins full of thread in rainbow colours all over the place. It is easy to imagine the noise and constant movement when the mill was in full production. Though many of the machines at the museum are not to do with this part of Derbyshire, they convey the same noise and clatter.

"The women partnering the thread
Were not just glamourous toys
As they kept those hungry frames well fed,
Despite the clamourous noise."

From a poem called 'The Ghost of Masson Mill, you can read there

The Yorkshire Loom is one of the machines you can see at the mills. These machines date back about 130 years. Up to five healds were moving at once and producing various weaves. The Shuttle travels about 60mph. A full shuttle lasts about seven minutes and produces about 13 inches (33cms) of cloth. There are also Jacquard Looms, using paper patterns and cotton doubling machines, producing piping cord, as well as many others.

Bobbins spools and (far left) a 'pirn' which fits into a shuttle

A Yorkshire Loom

Still a thriving site

A Jaquard loom with the pattern

Today you can buy gifts from the museum, including cloth, bobbins, pirns and multicoloured cord on wooden bobbins, all made on the historic equipment.
■ **Masson Mills Working Textile Museum, Derby Road, Matlock Bath, Derbyshire DE4 3PY01629 58100**
■ **www.massonmills.co.uk**

The Masson Mills shopping village mega store is sited in one of the later mills, with a variety of famous name shops, as well as a Riverside Restaurant. There is also an exhibition and conference facilities are available.
■ **Masson Mills 01629 760208**

Braids, balloons and bandages

During the war, Masson Mill turned out bandages, and also made material which was used for barrage balloons.

The Masson Mills were the oldest in the world to have been in continuous production when they closed in 1991. Many families in the area have had generations before them who have worked there.

At the mills is a leaflet from 1946, describing good working conditions and hours mon - fri 7.30am to 5.30pm and praising the canteen and the fortnightly tea dances in the canteen.

Powering still

When the mills were first built, the river's power was harnessed by a water wheel. Now a turbine is turned by the river's power. This supplies electricity to the Mills complex and to the National Grid, a good example of green energy!

A Warping Mill

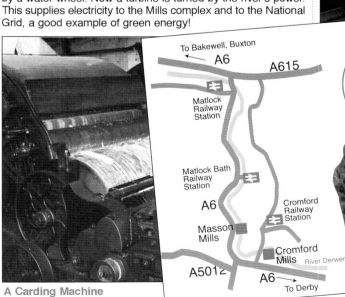

A Carding Machine

A bobbin of cord bought from the museum

A Cotton Doubling machine

William Gell

A local man whose was closely involved with the excavation work on Pompeii, Italy, in the 1820s. He made detailed drawings and plans of the site and wrote books on the subject

Sir William Gell (April 1 1777 - 4 Feb 1836), was born at Hopton in Derbyshire. He was a classical archeologist, who travelled extensively and produced exquisite drawings and plans of the places he visited.

Sir William Gell. Based on an 1816 portrait by Cornelius Varley

Early life

William was the son of Philip Gell and Dorothy Milnes, a family whose wealth was made in the lead mining industry.. He was educated at Derby School and then went to Cambridge.

In the early 1800s he travelled in Greece and some of the neighbouring islands. It was a diplomatic mission and on his return in he was knighted.

Gell the Dilettante

In 1807 he was elected a Member of the Society of Dilettanti and a Fellow of the Royal Society.

The Society of Dilettanti was a society of noblemen and gentlemen, which sponsored the study of ancient Greek and Roman art and the creation of new work in the style.

It began life as a dining club in London 1734, started by a group of people who had been on a 'Grand Tour'.

This tour around the world was a common pastime of the upper classes of the time.

The society was first led by Francis Dashwood and the members included several dukes. Members had to pay part of their income if they had a financially good year.

The group wanted to improve the artistic and intellectual tastes of the country and funded scholarships for young people to go on the Grand Tour, or on archeological expeditions..

Travels

In 1811 the Society of Dilettanti commissioned Gell to explore Greece and Asia Minor. These travels resulted in several publications, which became well known and respected in scholarly circles. He wrote of places such as Italy and Greece when these places were comparatively little known to English travellers and classical students. His works became standard texts and are still of use for archaeology students and others today.

Pompeiana

Some of Gell's best known work illustrated the progress of the excavation of Pompeii he was involved with in the 1820s.

In 1815 Gell settled in Naples, He obtained special permits for visiting the ongoing excavations at nearby Pompeii at all hours and so could keep a good record..He made detailed plans and views of the streets and houses as well as detailed descriptions:.

"The walls of the crypt are painted in large panels, alternately red and yellow, having in the centre of each some little figure or landscape ...Below these panels are smaller divisions, in which, on a black ground, are painted flowers, not unlike the lily in form, but generally of a red colour...." .

Much of the work was published in **Pompeiana; the Topography, Edifices and Ornaments of Pompeii,** his best known work. The artist J. P. Gandy helped with some of the lovely paintings in this. Gell's other works included Topography of Rome and its Vicinity, Topography of Troy and its Vicinity, and Geography and Antiquities of Ithaca.

Camera Lucida

Gell made sketches with the help of a Camera Lucida and these sketches were turned into detailed engraved prints.

The name "camera lucida" is Latin for "lit room" The camera lucida is a lightweight, portable device that does not require special lighting conditions.

In the simplest type of camera lucida, the artist looks down at the drawing surface through a half-silvered mirror tilted at 45 degrees.

This device creates a reflected view of the scene being studied horizontally in front of the artist onto the drawing surface.

Sir William Gell died at Naples on the 4th of February 1836. His numerous drawings of classical ruins and localities, are preserved in the British Museum and at Derbyshire Record Office in Matlock.

A copy of Gell's Pompeii and one of the illustrations in it

Hopton Hall

This lovely old hall is famous for the snowdrop display in the grounds. It was the ancestral home of the Gell family, who lived here for almost 500 years.

The hall began life as an Elizabethan manor house, built by Anthony Gell in 1576. It later became known as Hopton Hall.

Many changes were made by Anthony's great grandson Philip, around 1780, who wanted to make it look more modern and made changes in the Georgian style.

The vast estate was made smaller in 1978, when some of it was taken as land for the making of a new reservoir, Carsington Water.

In 1989 the rest of the hall and its land eventually left the Gell family when it was sold and the contents auctioned off.

In 1996 the hall again got new owners, who are now lovingly restoring the hall, and the 30 acres in which it now stands, to their former glory.

The grounds and gardens of the old hall had received little or no maintenance for approximately forty years, but since 1996 the owners have gradually cleared and restored the woodland and its walks.

Whilst doing so, they uncovered a vast bed of snowdrops which had lain dormant for many years. Aconites are also in abundance in the gardens at the same time of year.

A Laburnum Tunnel and a number of walks, as well as a small Arboretum and Pinetum have now been created in the gardens. Two ponds and a lake are other additions.

Also in the gardens at Hopton is a red brick crinkle crankle wall, built in the 18th century, which runs alongside the main road obscuring the hall from view.

Hopton Hall, once home to the Gell family

This type of wall is wavy, like a serpent, and the other name for this style of wall is a serpentine wall. The wall traps the rays and warmth of the sun to assist fruit growing. In this wallled garden there are two large rose gardens.

Most of the hall is used as holiday lets now, but in April May many people come to see the stunning carpet of snowdrops, and aconites.

The gardens are also open in July and August for people to visit the floral displays. The funds that are raised from these open days go towards the restoration of the gardens.

■ www.hoptonhall.co.uk
■ 01629 540923

Carsington

Between Wirksworth and Ashbourne and near Hopton, is the small village of Carsington.

The main employment and source of income for this village over the centuries was lead mining and traces of mining can still be seen.

Lead ore has been extracted in the Derbyshire area since at least the Roman occupation. Many 'pigs' of lead with Roman letters inscribed on them have been found. Most are marked LVTVD, an abbreviation of the name Lutudarum. This must have been a local place where the lead was from but no one now knows where this was. Some have speculated it may have been Carsington.

Roman pig of lead found in Matlock. Note the last four letters LVTVD

The church of St Margaret dates from the 12th century. It was largely rebuilt in 1648. Re-edified is another way of saying re-built and this word can be seen on a sundial on the church wall. This sundial is one of the oldest in Derbyshire.

Left: The church sundial

Carsington Water

Carsington was chosen as the site for a new reservoir and work began on this in 1979. Other places were considered but tis one was chosen as thought to be least disruptive to the life of the local community.

Also the availability of stone from local quarries for dam building and shoreline protection was a factor.

In 1984 part of the original dam collapsed, and so was levelled to its foundations, with a new one, to a new design being built instead.

This inevitably brought changes to the village, with more houses and a bypass being built to take construction traffic

The finished reservoir, known as Carsington Water, was opened by the Queen in 1992. It is England's ninth largest reservoir.

As well as providing water it has become a popular tourist attraction, with a Visitor Centre, exhibition, education centre restaurant, cafe and shops.

Outdoor activities offered include canoeing, cycling, fishing, water skiing and sailing.

It is a good place to watch birdlife and there are two bird hides. There are managed woodlands around the reservoir, a good habitat for local wildlife.

■ Carsington Water Visitor Centre - (01629) 540696

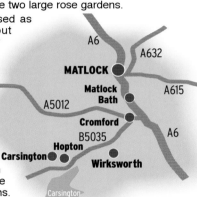

Bonsall

It was one of the Gell family who built the road known as the Via Gellia, around 1790. The name 'Via Gellia', is thought to derive from the Latin version of the name Gell. and the Latin word 'via' which means road or street.

The Via Gellia was built to provide transport for the lead ore from mines owned by the Gell family to the newly opened wharf at Cromford. It is a steep-sided, narrow, wooded valley running eastwards from Grangemill to Cromford.

"Via Gellia- Romantic scenery. Pools of water-Falls of water- lead works - paper mill."
A note about the Via Gellia rom The Gem of the Peak 1851

A road up from Via Gellia leads to Bonsall, an ancient former lead mining village.

A century and a half or so ago, Bonsall people were on the whole farmers, lead miners or working for the mills at Cromford and Via Gellia. Some people worked as frame knitters. Stockings were a major `cottage industry' and around 400 frame knitters set up in their homes. Their houses had long windows to admit the maximum day light to work by. Some of these type of windows can still be seen on some of the cottages

At the centre of the village is an interesting market cross with 13 steps in a conical form leading up to the slender cross shaft. It is said that John Wesley once preached at this cross.

Bonsall Brook flows toward Cromford where it was used to provide power for Richard Arkwright's mill.

The 13th century stone built St James's Church overlooks the village. The centre of the village is reached by the evocatively titled Clatterway.

Bonsall has an annual Well Dressing, usually in late July.

Viyella

The trade name Viyella, a corruption and shortening of the words Via Gellia, originated from the fabric that was produced by a company at one of the seven textile mills set in the valley.

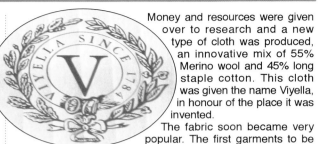

A Viyella shop in Harrogate

The company originated in a mill established in 1784 by the Hollins family. By 1851 the company was grand enough to show their products, including merino wools, cashmere and silk at the Great Exhibition in London.

The firm grew and in 1890 Henry Ernest Hollins doubled the capacity by purchasing a spinning mills at the Via Gellia.

Money and resources were given over to research and a new type of cloth was produced, an innovative mix of 55% Merino wool and 45% long staple cotton. This cloth was given the name Viyella, in honour of the place it was invented.

The fabric soon became very popular. The first garments to be made in the new fabric were men's shirts and nightshirts, but it was also used for blouses, night dresses, skirts and sheets. The name became internationally known and is still popular today.

Hen racing

Every August in the pub car park of the Barley Mow public house, Bonsall, is a bizarre event - the Hen Racing Championships. Anyone with a hen can enter, but only hens hatched and reared in Derbyshire are eligible to race. This is a popular activity and attracts the crowds eager to see the feathered athletes as they keep on cluckin!

Ready steady crow?

Alien tourists

At the start of the new millennium, Bonsall was given a taste of fame with some alleged visitors of the more extraterrestrial kind.

In October 2000, there were numerous sightings of UFOs reported over the village

There was also a short video, shot by a local resident, which was said to show footage of UFOs.

The press got hold of the UFO stories and enthusiasts have frequented Bonsall ever since hoping for a UFO sighting of their own.

The landlord of the Barley Mow conducts UFO walks and the pub is sometimes promoted as being the the 'U.F.O. Capital of Europe.'

Tufa Cottage

Nestling in the Via Gellia valley, near Bonsall, is Tufa Cottage which was built around 1830 as a game-keeper's cottage for the Gell Estate.

Tufa is a decorative porous limestone rock often used in Alpine beds and on Rock Gardens.

It is formed when lime from heavily mineralised water is deposited onto moss. The lime gradually builds up and forms a hard layer. When the moss decays, a porous rock is then left behind.

The cottage is built with this rock and is thought to be the only one of its type in England.

The tufa was quarried just above the Via Gellia.

Left: The unusual market cross at Bonsall with its thirteen circular steps

The Roundhouse

The Roundhouse at Ringinglow

Leaving the city of Sheffield on the Ringinglow Road towards the Peak District, you pass a strangely shaped old building standing guard...

The old building known locally as The Roundhouse is, in fact, octagonal in shape and has been a famous landmark for many a decade.

An old toll house

In the eighteenth and nineteenth centuries, many roads used to have turnpikes. These roads were kept in good condition with the money raised from the tolls or fees charged to use them. There was someone to collect these tolls at the tollbars and building were often put up at these points for the toll bar keeper to use. The Roundhouse is one such building.

It was built for the Barber Fields toll bar, about 1795. It is at the place where the road divides in different directions. It was the toll house to collect money on the old toll road we now know as Ringinglow Road. The Roundhouse is now a private residence. The toll gates are long gone.

Other toll houses

Some more of these old toll house buildings remain in Sheffield itself. One stands at Pitsmoor at the junction of Burngreave and Pitsmoor Road. Hunters Bar had a toll bar, hence the name, but the building is long gone.

Also at bottom of Collegiate Crescent as it meets Ecclesall Road the old toll house is still there on the right, now used as a shop.

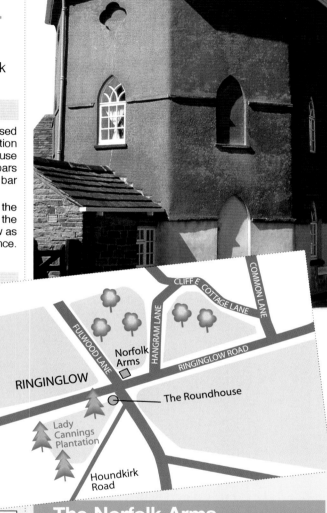

The old milestone in the car park wall and the pub frontage

The Norfolk Arms

Across the road from the Round House is the Norfolk Arms, where tired turnpike travellers would rest and get refreshments,

This characterful pub with its castle- like frontage is over 200 years old.

Set into the car park wall, there is an old milestone, stating that the distance to Sheffield town hall is 5 miles.

There is also a cute little Victorian post box.

The Sheffield Round Walk passes by here and the inn still refreshes many a weary traveller on wheels or foot.

The Ringinglow Roundhouse with (inset) the windows of the out-buildings

Ringinglow

Four legged residents

At Ringinglow are found two very unusual types of four legged creatures.

Near the junction with Fulwood Lane is a little toy shop packed with many delights - including some lovely wooden rocking horses. There are also doll's houses, mobiles, masks prams puppets and baby shoes.

■ Ringinglow Toys, Fulwood Lane, S11 7TS
■ Telephone: 0114 2302965
■ www.dapplegrey.co.uk

And a little further down Fulwood Lane you may do a double take as you spot some strange looking creatures grazing amongst the trees. Not sheep, cows or horses - but Alpacas.

These belong to Quicksaw Farm, home to Mayfield Alpacas.

Breeding these animals was first a hobby for Elaine H Sharp, but now it is a thriving business with around eighty Alpacas, a purpose designed building and a visitor centre, which has refreshment facilities.

The farm has an educational aspect and welcomes group visits.

■ Mayfield Alpacas, Fulwood Lane, Ringinglow Village, S10 4LH.
■ Telephone: 0114 263 0033
■ Mobile: 0771 365 6301
■ e mail: info@mayfieldalpacas.com
■ www.mayfieldalpacas.com

Ringinglow Toys on Fulwood Lane

The Alpacas at Mayfield Alpacas graze in the sunshine

Across the road from the Roundhouse you can join the Sheffield Round Walk, leading down the Limb Valley into Whirlow Brook Park

The well worn paths

The view out from the beginning of the Houndkirk Road rough track near Ringinglow

Wildflowers at the side of the Houndkirk Road

Hollow ways and turnpikes

If you take the road in front of the Roundhouse, which is leading out directly in front of the Norfolk Arms, you are on walking on Houndkirk Road. This old pack horse route carries on as a rougher track, leading off the road to the right.

The Houndkirk Road was another toll road, the Buxton Turnpike, which led out across the moors to Buxton, via Fox House and Grindleford.

These toll roads would have pack horse trains carrying salt over from Cheshire to Sheffield and going the other way would be the cutlery from Sheffield or lead, wool and millstones from the Peak District.

The turnpikes took the easiest routes over the moors which had been well worn by people and horses. Some were paved and some were worn so deep that they made grooves in the landscape, known as hollow ways. Many in this area converge in a very deeply cut line near Burbage Brook and Longshaw, known as Hollowgate. This is pictured below.

A fake city

Views around the Houndkirk Road in August, with the heather in full bloom

Fire and bullets

If you had walked the moorlands at Burbage and Houndkirk in 1940, it would not have been the quiet area you find today. Instead you would have found the moors a busy place full of soldiers and activity, for they were used as a major player in World War Two defence - as the site for an imitation city.

There would have been trenches, ditches, platforms and lights, making up a decoy city to draw the German bombers away from Sheffield and it's prize targets - the steelworks.

This was one of six decoy cities built in the area, but only traces of one here and at Curbar Gap remain.

To create a convincing city, an artist was flown over Sheffield and made drawings of the layout. These were then used to create the decoy city and represent a marshalling yard, streets and steelworks. The supposed steelworks were created with controlled fires in oil filled trenches. Theatrical lights created the glow of furnaces opened to pour molten steel. Fires were also used to simulate burning, bombed buildings and the sparks of electric trams were simulated.

The decoy city was manned by soldiers billeted at nearby Dore. When on duty there they would camp overnight.

A bomb proof control bunker was built at the highest point of the moor. From here the soldiers could look out for enemy aircraft. Attack warnings were relayed by wireless as they waited, sitting as bait for the bombs.

The platform for this control bunker, an access track for vehicles and some ditches and banks are all that is left of the huge decoy city today, but they may be hard to spot.

Soldiers carried out training on the moors too, and some earthfast boulders in the area bear bullet hole marks or mortar scars. Perhaps some of these soldiers left the moors to take part in the all too real action elsewhere and never returned.

Dad's Army

The local Home Guard also did some training out near Ringinglow. Another place they used was a rifle range at Totley. My father was in the Home Guard and remembers being taken out in a van on Sundays, after a week of toiling at the steelworks. He and others in their ill-fitting uniforms were given a rifle, and spent time firing at targets to improve their ability to shoot and so protect us from any potential invaders!

Houndkirk Road

A long trodden way

The Houndkirk Road, built in 1758 as the Sheffield to Buxton Turnpike, is a fabulous place to enjoy the open views and wildness that we are lucky enough to have so close to us - and so easily accessible too. The heather in summer is stunning and the sense of space uplifting.

The route was once trodden by packhorse trains in medieval times, then carriages rumbled along its cobbled surface in the 19th century. Some local people call it 'the Roman road' and maybe this way over the moors was used as far back as that, no one can be sure.

The road winds over the moors like a light brown, dusty snake. It leads to Fox House, where it joins the main Sheffield to Hathersage Road, with the Fox House Inn a little way ahead on the right.

Edith and The Sheik

From the imagination of a timid Derbyshire 'pig farmer's wife' came a steamy tale of abduction and lust, which sent shockwaves though the roaring twenties

One of the most steamy early films, The Sheik, which made Rudolf Valentino a sex symbol, began its life in a quiet Derbyshire village, penned by a quiet and unassuming woman named Edith.

Country living

It was in Hazelwood, Derbyshire that a respectable, unremarkable lady called Edith Maude Winstanley (née Henderson), lived. She later became known as E.M. Hull, the pseudonym she used when writing the novel which was to bring her a lot of rather unwanted publicity.

Edith was born in London, in Hampstead, in 1880, on the 16th of August.

She was the only daughter of a shipowner, James Henderson. Edith travelled a lot due to her fathers job connections. One place she went to was Algeria, which may have set the seeds of imagination for her later tale.

In 1899 she married a man called Percy Winstanley Hull, from Hazelwood, but working in London, which is where they met.

At first they lived in Surrey, before venturing back to Percy's roots in the first decade of the last century, when they moved into Percy's childhood home, at Hazelwood.

It was a respectable, grand house called 'The Knowle' with large gardens. They had one daughter to share it with.

Percy Hull was an agriculturalist noted as a good pig breeder, and their home and lifestyle added up to the perfect country idyll.

Novel notoriety

Perhaps this ladylike rural existence was a little staid for Edith, who had travelled and lived in London.

Maybe this is why she began making up and writing down stories, to travel in her imagination at least.

She did say in later years that she had started writing because she was lonely when her husband was away during the First World War, which is when The Sheik, her first novel, was penned..

Without much expectation, Edith sent the book to a publisher. They liked it and so it was printed in 1919.

The Sheik tells the tale of an impetuous and spoilt (and later seemingly masochistic), young woman called Diana Mayo. Travelling alone with just local tribesmen for escort, she heads off into the desert in search of adventure.

What she does get is kidnapped, by the charismatic but brutal Sheik Ahmed Ben Hassan. He had taken a fancy to her earlier, at a party in a hotel in the town she has now left behind, along with the niceties of society.

Flung onto The Sheik's horse and whisked across the desert, Diana is held captive in Ahmed's tent.

At first she puts up resistance but then succumbs to his manly strength as he repeatedly ravishes her amidst the purple prose:

'The flaming light of desire burning in his eyes turned her sick and faint. Her body throbbed with the consciousness of a knowledge that appalled her, and each separate nerve in her system shrank against the understanding that had come to her under the consuming fire of his ardent gaze, and in the fierce embrace that was drawing her shaking limbs closer and closer to the man's own pulsating body - "Oh you brute! You brute!" she wailed, until his kisses silenced her.'

Hazelwood

Belper

A517

A6   **A38**

B5023

Duffield

A52

A38   **Derby**

'The Sheik' Ahmed Ben Hussan. The role was played by star Rudolph Valentino in a film version of the book

A hit and a backlash

Critics condemned the book as pornography, but as is often the case with adverse publicity, it did even better and the public lapped it up, especially women.

The book is extremely politically uncorrect looking back on it today and would cause just as much publicity for very different reasons probably..

At the time it was published, the novel was said to have 'brazen physicality' and was shocking to many of the people who dipped into its pages, with the steamy passages of wanton lust and helpless desire:

"His dark passionate eyes burnt into her like a hot flame. His encircling arms were like bands of fire, scorching her. His touch was torture. Helpless, like a wild, trapped thing, she lay against him, panting, trembling, her wide eyes fixed on him, held against their will. Fascinated she could not turn them away and the image of the brown, handsome face, with its flashing eyes, straight cruel mouth and strong chin seemed searing into her brain."

Diana seems almost masochistic in her reactions at times:

"His arms held her like a vice hurting her, but they felt like heaven"
but in spite of his appalling behaviour, Diana is attracted to Ahmed and he is described in romantic, hero-like phrases:

"A picturesque, barbaric figure with floating robes and great white cloak, the profile of his lean face clean cut against the evening sky."

Diana's imprisonment is made to sound almost enjoyable at times too, with attention from a French valet Gaston, who is a dab hand at coffee and lemonade and brings magazines.

The tent has nice bookcases and co-ordinating furnishings, making it clear that The Sheik has a good taste in interior decor, as well as a splendid physique and well kept fingernails. It is a very romanticised view of what amounts to abuse.

But Diana's attraction to and, finally, love for, the testosterone charged Sheik, is made all ok in the end.

To suit the mood and climate of the times, we find he is in fact the long lost son of an English aristocrat (like Tarzan was) .

Ahmed's father is, in fact, the Earl of Glencaryll and his mother a spanish noblewoman, who ran away at 17 to the desert, to escape from an unhappy marriage. She was pregnant and ended up staying with Ahmed's father to have the child, whom he adopted as his own son.

Edith's novel is credited with starting the hugely popular "desert-romance" genre.

Some people have wondered if Mrs Hull was inspired by the exploits (in suitably charismatic attire of flowing white embroidered robes) of T. E. Lawrence, better known as Lawrence of Arabia. Lawrence had become a popular and romanticiesd figure after his activities during the time of the first World War and had initiated an interest for many people about Arabia.

It is hard to know if this is so and how much Edith would have known or heard about Lawrence when she began her own story.

MRS. E. M. HULL
DEATH OF WELL-KNOWN NOVELIST

The death occurred on Tuesday after a short illness, at her home, Holmeside, Hazelwood, of Mrs. Edith Maude Hull, the famous novelist and writer of desert stories.

Mrs. Hull travelled extensively in Europe, also in America, Canada, India and later she made four journeys into the Sahara Desert to collect local colour for her novels.

Her books commanded a wide public, especially in America and in Europe, where "The Sheik" was translated into fourteen languages.

Other well-known books by

MRS. E. M. HULL

Hollywood

The book became a huge success and so quickly attracted the attention of the film makers of Hollywood. A film based on the novel was made, starring a new filmstar of the time, Rudolph Valentino. Rudolph was a young Italian who had just been shot to stardom a few months earlier after dancing a steamy tango in the film Four Horsemen of The Apocalypse.

The film of The Sheik was a huge success too, and made a star of the leading man, Valentino, who became known as 'The Great Lover' of the silent screen.

His exotic portrayal of the wilful seducer in The Sheik sealed his reputation. The smouldering stare that seemed to imply much more than ever could be shown on the silent screen was a hit with many.

Valentino died young (31), in 1926. His death had a big enough impact to cause mass hysteria and some women even committed suicide at the news. The untimely end helped form a legend.

The film had made Edith into even more of a celebrity too, but a very reluctant one.

The Sheik was first shown in Derby in 1923 but she was not there to see it as she was in North Africa with her daughter, E. M Hull wrote a factual book about this trip - Camping in the Sahara (1926).

She wrote seven other novels, including The Shadow of the East (1921), The Sons of the Sheik (1925) - again adapted as a Valentino film - The Lion Tamer (1928) and The Forest of Terrible Things (1939).

Edith Maude Hull Winstanley died on Tuesday 11 February, 1947, after a short illness.

Her Grave is at Hazelwood Church. Nothing on the cruciform monument reminds us of her unexpected notoriety, as it is a memorial to Edith the respectable farmer's wife, not the E.M. Hull the public fastened on to after her exotic and controversial book

An anecdotal letter in the Derbyshire Advertiser, June 30th 1972, about Mrs. E M Hull The letter is by someone who knew her and who is replying to an earlier article:

"That distinguished journalist Claud Cockburn has been having fun in the pages of The Observer at the expense of E.M, Hull, author of 'The Sheik' and other bestselling romantic novels of the twenties.

Having known Mrs Hull in the days when she and her husband and their daughter lived in Hazelwood, I feel bound to come to her defence.

Mrs Hull was a modest, gentle, clever woman who wrote her books to make money for her family. She was unlucky over contracts and film rights and others reaped large fortunes from her hard working authorship. Her books are still being published and enjoyed by a large public, In fact 'The Sheik' is about to gallop through a new serialisation in Australia.

She never spoke of her writing but she was what I would call a 'good trouper' and her books were no more superficial than other romantic novels of the period.......what I want to put on record is that I am glad to have known Mrs Hull, a hardworking professional author if ever there was one and certainly not a purveyor of dirty books."

Randolph Douglas

Most people have heard of Houdini - but how many know of Randini, Sheffield's own aspiring escapologist, a friend of the great man himself ?

From a private collection

Randolph Osborne Douglas was a talented and amazing man. He began life wanting to be an escapologist, like his hero Houdini, but health problems ended this dream. Instead he found other ways to channel his creativity, becoming a talented silversmith, artist and model maker, as well as running a quirky museum.

Sheffield boy with a headful of dreams

Randolph was born in Norton, Sheffield (then in Derbyshire) on March 31st 1895. He was from a fairly wealthy, very artistic family.

His mother, Margaret (maiden name Osborne) was a painter and his father, Robert Strachan Douglas, originally from Edinburgh, was a talented and prolific silversmith, modeller and designer.

When Randolph was just 15, his mother died. It was on the same day as the ninth birthday of Randolph's little sister Margaret.

With both children young and in need of continuing security, his father remarried, to Margaret's sister Catherine.

Catherine and Robert had another child, Ambrose and the family moved from Norton to a house at Carrington Road, Sheffield.

It seems that Randolph's interest in escapology started very early in life. but at first was an apprentice silversmith, working with his father. This was overtaken by his passion for the more magical arts.

His sister, Margaret was sometimes tied up by him as he tried out knots and escapes. One of his notebooks lists the money he had spent on locks, handcuffs and a straitjacket in 1911, when he was sixteen - not the usual type of haul for a schoolboy.

He used to buy locks from the saturday 'rag' market in Sheffield and built up a collection, turning half of his his small attic bedroom at Carrington Road into a tiny museum.

Randolph invented stage shows and tricks for himself, calling himself 'The Great Randolph, or 'Randin.' These ideas had macabre titles such as The Death Chamber and were often full of detailed notes for his proposed career in Houdini's footsteps.

Randolph also made exquisite drawings in his notebooks, depicting the shows of other magicians he had seen at the Empire and Hippodrome, which he got autographed by the performers.

A drawing by 'The Great Randolph'

Courtesy of/copyright of Buxton Museum and Art Gallery

Left: Randolph with his parents and sister in 1907
From a private collection

Empire inspiration?

Photographs in the Douglas Collection, now at Buxton Museum and Art Gallery, show him trussed in an alarmingly heavy looking array of chains and padlocks. They were taken in 1913 and 1914, the sensitive looking teenager striking poses as he tries on his new persona, as 'The Great Randin'.

Considering the young Randolph's passion for escapology, it is highly likely that when the American 'handcuff king' Harry Houdini came to the Sheffield Empire, in January 1904, that the young pretender, then just nine, was taken along.

It was on January 19th that Houdini did his usual publicity stunt of escaping from the local police cells. In Sheffield the court, police station and cells (clocktower shown above right) were at Water Lane, near Sheffield markets. The cell which Houdini escaped from was the one which had once held the notorious murderer Charlie Peace. To prove his feat, he was given a certificate by the police.

PRISON BREAKING EXTRAORDINARY HOUDINI ESCAPES FROM A TRIPLE LOCKED CELL
Certificate:
"This is to certify that Mr Harry Houdini was this day stripped stark naked and locked in the cell which once contained Charlie Peace."
At the Empire last night Houdini freed himself from several pairs of handcuffs more than one pair of which were of peculiar design and won enthusiastic applause from a crowded house."

Sheffield and Rotherham Independent January 20, 1904

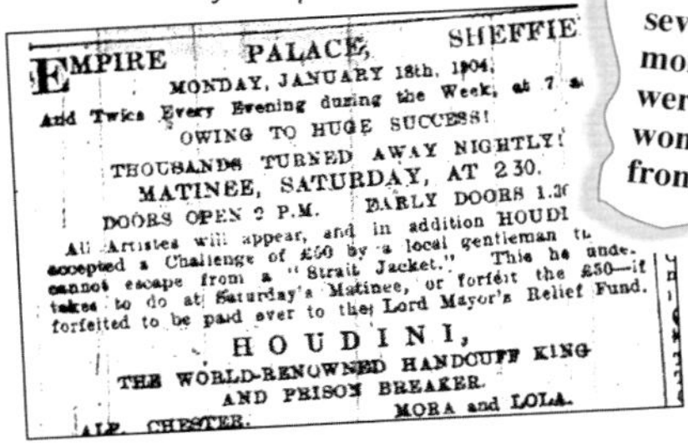

EMPIRE PALACE, SHEFFIE
MONDAY, JANUARY 18th, 1904.
And Twice Every Evening during the Week, at 7
OWING TO HUGE SUCCESS!
THOUSANDS TURNED AWAY NIGHTLY!
MATINEE, SATURDAY, AT 2.30.
DOORS OPEN 2 P.M.   EARLY DOORS 1.30
All Artistes will appear, and in addition HOUDI
accepted a Challenge of £50 by a local gentleman th
cannot escape from a "Strait Jacket." This he unde-
takes to do at Saturday's Matinee, or forfeit the £50—if
forfeited to be paid over to the Lord Mayor's Relief Fund.
HOUDINI,
THE WORLD-RENOWNED HANDCUFF KING
AND PRISON BREAKER.
ALF. CHESTER.   MORA and LOLA.

A report in the local newspaper tells of the enthusiastic crowd at the Empire. Maybe Randolph was one of them.

Douglas corresponded with Houdini from around 1913 and according to a transcript of an interview with his sister Margaret, in the archives at Buxton Museum, the Empire is where they first met. Houdini knew that Randolph was no ordinary fan, with his knowledge of locks and stage magic. The two became friends and whenever Houdini performed at the theatre in Sheffield, Randolph went backstage to help. Randin began to sign himself 'Randini.'

Margaret also said in her interview that Randolph 'passed on illusions' to Houdini, but would never take any money for them.

Photo: Sheffield Newspapers archives

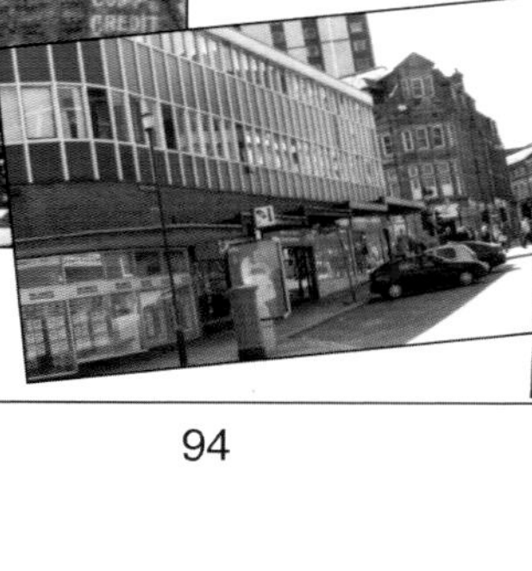

The Empire Theatre, Sheffield, which stood on the corner of Charles Street and Pinstone Street and (right) the site today

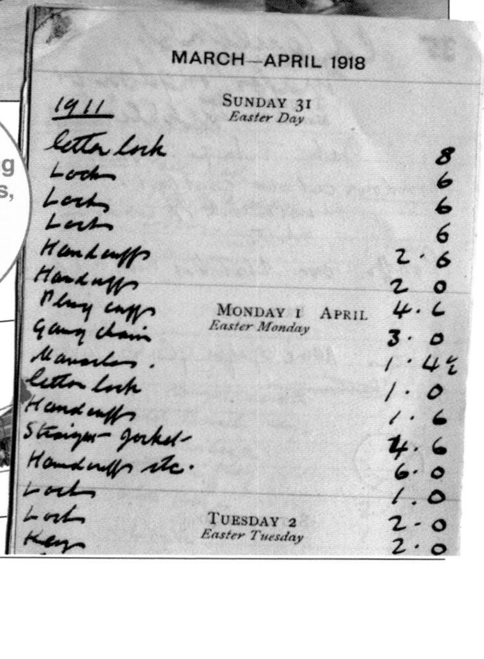

Randolph Douglas aka Randini, looks surprisingly comfortable in an array of restraints

Courtesy of/ copyright of Buxton Museum and Art Gallery

Right: Randolph's notebook showing purchase of locks, handcuffs and 'straight jacket'
From a private collection

MARCH—APRIL 1918

1911
letter lock   8
lock   6
lock   6
lock   6
Handcuffs   2.6
Handcuffs   2.0
SUNDAY 31
Easter Day
Play cuffs   4.6
Gang chain   3.0
Manacles.   1.4½
letter lock   1.0
Handcuffs   1.6
MONDAY 1 APRIL
Easter Monday
Strainger jacket   4.6
Handcuffs etc.   6.0
Lock   1.0
Lock   2.0
Key   2.0
TUESDAY 2
Easter Tuesday

94

An iconic escape trick

It is obvious from other notes. letters and postcards between Randolph and Houdini, held both in Buxton Museum and at the Magic Circle in London, that they became close friends.

"Ever since I was thirteen years of age," he said, "I have been fascinated by the mechanism of locks and other things, and every lock I could get hold of I used to dissect it and assemble it again. Hundreds have passed through my hands, and from that stage I turned to handcuffs, and so on. When I first met Houdini - I was living in Sheffield at the time - he soon realised that I was not the usual type of 'fan' or autograph hunter, and I think I impressed him with my knowledge of locks and the art of escapology".
Randolph speaking to a reporter in a newspaper cutting from 'The Worlds Fair' Saturday May 28th 1938

"Randolph had done a drawing of Houdini's torture chamber, and method of working, based on what he had seen the previous night when sitting among the audience. Houdini was astounded, and admitted that my son had correctly interpreted the secret of the trick, and he was so interested that he begged the drawing for a memento".

The friendship grew and Houdini visited his young friend Randolph at his Sheffield home whenever he could.

It even seems that one of Houdini's most iconic escapes began life in this young boy's attic at Carrington Road.

On one visit, after taking tea, Houdini was taken up to the attic. Here, Randolph's (step) mother proceeded to help her son become suspended from a beam in the ceiling, whilst fastened in a straitjacket.

Randolph then did an upside down escape, shedding from his cocoon like bindings.

"Houdini was again impressed, and it was not long afterwards that he started with the trick in America."
Source as above

So Houdini's fame spread, with one of his most famous spectacles inspired by an unassuming boy from Sheffield.

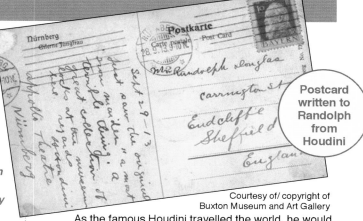

Postcard written to Randolph from Houdini

Courtesy of/ copyright of Buxton Museum and Art Gallery

As the famous Houdini travelled the world, he would send his friend postcards at his home in Sheffield.

One postcard, written by Houdini from Nuremberg on September 28 1913, (dated 29th by Houdini),says:

"Just saw the original 'iron maiden' a most terrible thing. A great collection of locks at the museum here. Regards, H Houdini. Appollo Theatre Nuremberg".

From America, Germany, London and the provinces cards arrived from Houdini, yet the only evidence of Randolph's travels are around Derbyshire.

He did go to a camp near Durham when he was called up in the First World War, in January 1916. When at the camp he and Houdini kept up their correspondence.

Randolph's service was short lived however, when health problems were discovered, a weak heart, that made him unfit for duty. He was discharged in October 1916.

Some of Randolph's locks From a private collection

Courtesy of/copyright of Buxton Museum and Art Gallery

Randolph (right) and a fellow soldier, when he was in the army, in July 1916 From a private collection

A record of a grand career

Monday, January 10th, 1921.

CINEMA HOUSE,
(The Picture Play House)
FARGATE, SHEFFIELD.
Continuous Programme, 1.15 to 10.15.

Proprietors—
The Sheffield & District Cinematograph Theatres Ltd.
Box Office Phone 1382.
Resident Manager - Mr. J. R. DOWNING.

(5) THE AMAZING QUEST OF
MR. ERNEST BLISS.

No. 2.—The Greengrocer.

This adventure, complete in itself, offers
a great rarity—a genuinely funny British
comedy. Mary Brough is exquisitely good.

• • • •

(6) THE GRIM GAME.

Featuring Houdini, the "Handcuff King."

Known all over the world as a self-
liberator, illusionist, and magician, Houdini
has been a star on the halls for years past.
By methods of his own, he has repeatedly
mystified police and public officials by
escaping from handcuffs, strait-jackets,
locked safes, death cells, chains and roped
boxes. This picture shows him doing all
he knows in his own line, and tells a most
interesting story into the bargain.

Randolph kept scrapbooks with articles, flyers, programmes etc. about Harry Houdini and followed his adventures closely from his home in Carrington Road.

He would more than likely have seen Houdini's venture into film, The Grim Game, which played Sheffield in January 1921. Houdini posted Randolph some photo stills from the movie.

The last entry in Randolph's autograph book is by Harry Houdini, in March 1920. This was the last time that Houdini came to Sheffield.

Randolph's Houdini scrapbooks
Courtesy of/copyright of Buxton Museum and Art Gallery

To Randolph Douglas
In remembrance of my 8th visit to Sheffield April 27/99

"safe Bind, Safe Find. does not apply to the undersigned"

Harry Houdini

278 W. 113 St

Houdini's entries in Randolph's autograph book
Courtesy of/copyright of The Magic Circle Archives

As the years go by, the pastings in Randolph's scrapbook become less, maybe because Randolph was too busy with other things. The last entries are newspaper cuttings about Houdini's death, on Halloween, in 1926.

Sheffield march 17-1920

Today sixteen years ago I chewed and escaped from the dreaded mirror Handcuff at London Hippodrome, and Jan 19 - 1904 I conquered the famous Charles Peace Cell here in Sheffield at Pobes Head Quarters

Houdini

EMPIRE, SHEFFIELD
MONDAY, 15th MARCH, 1920
6.30. TWICE NIGHTLY. 8.30.
MATINEE THURSDAY, AT 2.30.

The World-Famous Self-Liberator

HOUDINI
(Himself).

BABUSIO BROS., Comedy Acrobats.
WILLIE ROLLS, He Does.
WE THREE, Music, Gowns and Comedy.
JOCK McKAY, Scots Comedian.
C. H. SCOTLAND, In Song, Comedy, Etc.
JOHN, HARRY and BURTON LESTER,
The Original "Jazz Boys."

Pree - List Entirely Suspended.
No Booking by Telephone.
Box Office Open Daily, 10 a.m. to 10 p.m.

HIPPODROME
To-night at 6.30
COTT ... FIELD

Sheffield Empire Palace
... ES STREET and PINSTONE STREET.
MR. H. SIDEBOTHAM. Telephone No. 669

PROGRAMME
MONDAY, MAR. 15th, 1920
TWICE NIGHTLY AT 6-30 AND 8-30.

(A) ... Orchestra
1—OVERTURE
Musical Director ... Mr. ARTHUR GRIMMETT.

2 FIRST APPEARANCE IN ENGLAND
AFTER SIX YEARS OF
The World-famous SELF-LIBERATOR
HOUDINI ... (Himself)

3 Latest News Pictures

4 BABUSIO BROS.
Patter Comedy Acrobats and Tumblers

5 WILLIE ROLLS - He does?

"It was a labour of love fostered by friendship," said *Mr. Douglas.*

From an article in The Worlds Fair' Saturday May 28th 1938

CHALLENGE
Houdini, Sheffield Empire

The above Challenge has been Accepted by
HOUDINI
for the Second House, Friday Night, at
Sheffield Empire, April 25th,

Harry Houdini and Randolph Douglas outside the Empire Theatre Sheffield in 1920
Courtesy of/copyright of Buxton Museum and Art Gallery

Diverse Talents

Randolph, unable to be a stage performer and escapologist due to his poor health, needed to follow another path.

He made made money later in life from another of his diverse talents, as a model maker, making unbelievably tiny models for promoting various firms, including a tiny chair and lamp for a dentist and miniature saws for a tool manufacturer. He also made large scale models for factories.

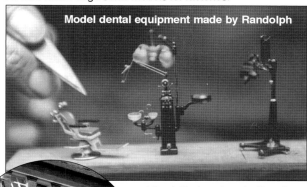

Model dental equipment made by Randolph

His letterheads at the time describe him as 'maker of better models' and 'specialist in scale models reproduced in miniature for educational, exhibition and publicity purposes."

His employment also included working at John Rounds and Son, Tudor Street, Sheffield (this was near where the Crucible Theatre is now) and also at silversmiths Cooper Brothers, Arundel Street, Sheffield. The Cooper Buildings still survive as part of the Sheffield Science Park (pictured).

A new phase

It was at Cooper Brothers that Randolph met his future wife, Hetty Bown, from Weston Street, Walkley, who worked in the warehouse there. They were married on March 31st, Randolph's birthday, in 1926.

Their marital home was a pretty cottage they had purchased in the village of Castleton. Here they lived, but it was no ordinary home, as it was also home to a small museum where Randolph displayed his many wonderful, quirky and exotic acquisitions, the House of Wonders.

Randolph in his attic 'museum' at Carrington Road
From a private collection

Model of Speedwell Cavern by Randolph Private collection

Model cottages that are also match holders. Made by Randolph for his nieces
From a private collection

Randolph (right) with his wife Hetty and a friend. The couple were both keen cavers Private collection

Randolph and Hetty on another outing, possibly at Ingleton Private collection

The House of Wonders

THE DOUGLAS MUSEUM
THE HOUSE OF WONDERS

Under the gaze of Peveril Castle in Castleton, in an area known as the Stones, was the cottage that was home to Randolph, Hetty and The Douglas Museum.

The couple lived in one part of the cottage, and the other half they turned into their House of Wonders. The museum became a popular tourist attraction, with curious visitors being shown around by torchlight, for a sixpenny fee.

As well as Randolph's amazing collection of locks, there were zulu masks, fossils, clay pipes, minerals, padlocks, handcuffs, butterflies, spears...an endless and eclectic variety

Another item was a model, sent by his friend Harry Houdini from Nuermberg, of the "Iron Maiden" a form of torturing instrument which encased the victim and plunged iron spikes into his or her body. Naturally, Houdini was deeply interested in anything of this nature and so he knew was Mr. Douglas.

TELEGRAPH August 2nd 1935

SHEFFIELD TELE[GRAPH]

Derbyshire.

COTTAGE WITH MANY TREASURES.

A Museum in Miniature.

CASTLETON CRAFTSMAN'S REMARKABLE SKILL.

Derbyshire villages hold many surprises. They remind one of those lucky [...]

Two models of the Douglas Museum at Castleton, made by Randolph. They are shown about actual size
From private collections

A model of the ropewalk in Peak Cavern, Castleton, by Randolph
From a private collection

A foil picture of Peveril Castle

YOUNG SHEFFIELDER OUTRIVALS LILLIPUT
MINIATURE MARVELS. FLOWERS IN A TOM THUMB GREENHOUSE

...A young Sheffielder, now living at Castleton, has taken up modelmaking for business firms, wealthy Americans and others. He is Mr. R.O.Douglas and he can make a model of anything from a battleship to a sewing machine.
He showed the writer a greenhouse so small that it will stand comfortably on one's thumb, yet it is complete down to the tiniest flowerpot. Looking through the glass of the house the rows of flower pots and blooms can be plainly seen.

Fascination of Detail
Then there is a model of Ann Hathaway's cottage at Stratford on Avon, drawn exactly to scale - 1 inch to 16 feet - which means that the building is reduced nearly 200 times. Yet not a detail is missing, every flower is there in the garden, and even the separate bushes which comprise the hedge can be distinguished.
Ever since he was a lad Mr. Douglas has been fascinated by the making of tiny models. "The detail work appeals to me," he said, "I am never satisfied unless I have included everything

Sheffield Daily Independent
Wednesday 29th June 1927

Randolph used to make items to sell in the museum, as souvenirs. As well as small models of the museum, these included exquisite pictures made from coloured foil placed under a line drawing done on glass.

Randolph's box of foil pieces for making his pictures
From a private collection

Right: The tiny greenhouse, now minus roof, sitting comfortably on the author's thumb
Courtesy Buxton Museum and Art Gallery

The wonder lives on

Randolph and Hetty ran their amazing museum together until Randolph's death on December 5th, 1956. He was buried at the Castleton church of St Edmund's.

After that Hetty continued to run the place and show people around, though as she got older she could not get to the upstairs part of the museum due to bad arthritis. People who visited the museum remember Hetty sitting knitting and welcoming the visitors..

Hetty died on April 21st, 1978, and was buried at St Edmund's, re-united with her fascinating and talented husband.

With the couple gone, the House of Wonders came to an end. The museum was closed, the marvels boxed and the cottage sold.

Remembering Randolph

Although Randolph's close friend Houdini is as famous as he ever was, Randolph's name and work is hardly known or remembered.

Castleton Information Centre is bringing Randolph Douglas back into the limelight however, and has an interesting display about him, with photographs and some of his models. including Ann Hathaway's Cottage.

◼ Castleton Information Centre, Main Street, Castleton, Hope Valley S33 8WP
◼ Telephone: (01433) 620679

The Douglas Museum contents were in the main taken up by Buxton Museum and Art Gallery, who display the collection at intervals, though some items, models etc. are held in private collections.
◼ Buxton Museum and Art Gallery, Terrace Road, Buxton, Derbyshire, SK17 6DU ◼ Tel: (01298) 24658

A flyer for the museum. Below, the 'smallest electric motor in the world' and 'a wonder in carving' - tongs made from a single match

Randolph in his early twenties

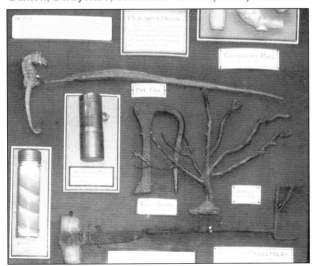

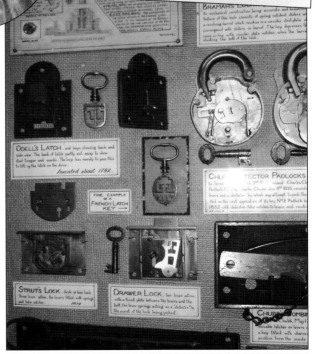

Above, a case of curiosities and (right) A case of locks from the Douglas Museum, now held at Buxton Museum and Art Gallery, though The collection is not always on display

◼ The author is working on a forthcoming biography of Randolph Douglas and his House of Wonders. If you have any information or recollections you would like to contribute please contact her via the publishers of this book, Pickard Communications

Some Peak inspired poems

ROPEMAKER'S RESTING PLACE

A tiny flame flickers in the darkness.
Like the soul of the man still burning.
The man whose nimble fingers
twisted the loop.
Stretching into the past
A line of twine and blood.
Rope born to haul miners,
tie gins, bless brides.
Tying the endless generations
together

Bert Marrison

A rock roof cradles the old walks
that surround his last home.
Below him the labrynthine world
has been a place
for a monks mystic tale,
and banquets of beggars.
A poet has wooed his sweetheart
Voices have echoed in song
Writers have searched for wonders
and has the Blue John beast prowled?

Some have dreamed of shells there,
pondering the origins of us all,
over frozen creatures coiled and twisted-
brief knots of life dotted forever
in the solid rock

Did others bring burning torches millennia ago
casting shadows on hands that drew
on damp glistening wall
totems of limbs and tusk now lost?
Did Norman children peer into the dark
and dare one another to enter?

Below him cavers crawl the depths
and visitors shuffle with craned neck
or stooped back.
Tied together by time's thread
they have all passed through.
And the flame flickers.

Notes: Ropemaker resting place

The man whose nimble fingers twisted the loop.
A man called Abraham Marrison used a now standard way of tying
off rope when finished, called the Marrison Loop. A candle burns
for his ancestor, ropemaker Bert Marrison, in The Peak Cavern
(Devils Arse) at Castleton. He worked there until his death in 1983,
using this same loop method.

bless brides
It was a tradition to give newlyweds in Castleton a washing line of rope

a monks mystic tale,
A monk named Gervaise of Tilbury wrote about the cavern in
1211.He told a tale of a shepherd who went into it looking for a lost
animal and came out in another, hidden sunlit land

banquets of beggars.
A banquet for beggars was held in the main cave in 1621.
This inspired poet Ben Jonson to write his poem
The Gypsies Metamorphos'd, about this event and the cavern

A poet has wooed his sweetheart
Lord Byron went on a boat trip in the cavern with his then sweetheart and wrote about it in his memoirs i the 1820s

Voices have echoed in song
Choirs of children used to hide in the darkness and then sing to
entertain surprised visitors. Concerts are still occasionally held in
the cavern.

Writers have searched for wonders
The Peak Cavern was one of the so called 'Seven Wonders of the
Peak', written about by various writers, including Michael Drayton,
William Camden, Thomas Hobbes and Daniel Defoe

And has the Blue John beast prowled?
Arthur Conan Doyle, the creator of famous sleuth Sherlock Holmes,
wrote about a monster living in a large cavern terrorising locals. His
book was called The Terror Of Blue John Gap

Some have dreamed of shells there,
Charles Darwin's grandfather, Erasmus Darwin, visited the cavern
and was inspired to evolutionary theories by seeing the fossils. He
came up with a phrase bout it: 'E conchis omnia' (everything from shells)

CIRCLES

WONDERING

Two walkers stand lost in thought.
Whose hands dragged these stones
as muscles ached and brow burst
with sweat?
Once a place of worship, they muse,
circle of spirit and stone
washed by skylarks song.

Or maybe a place of sacrifice,
with wide eyed virgins
awaiting their fate
as dawn's light heralds a feast.
Perhaps a place for wayward heifers,
lowing cattle snuffling rock.

Did ancient man tell times round
by shadow and sun, they wonder,
starmap the passing of the years
with these stony markers.

Bemused, they move on,
swords swaying and beating armour
as leather sandals turn up dust
in the still summer air.

Nine Ladies stone circle

Arbor Low stone circle

WAITING

The walker sits leaning against
the cool rock and dreams of others
who have rested here.
Lost in thought a red flutter catches his eye.
Coat filled by breeze she stands by the circle.
Their eyes meet.
Wisps of hair cover her face.
I wonder he thinks.
I wonder she thinks
Nothing said.
He may as well have been a ghost.

WATCHING

A plane sweeps above the circle
like times arrow
On a nearby edge bright figures clamber
hung from ropes like lycra spiders.
The hum of cars escaping the city
drifts on the air, breaking the silence.
Two walkers stand lost in thought.

HOPEFUL SMILERS

They line the roof grinning down at the passers by
A terrier-like terror with feathered wings
A mouth puller and a screamer

Wordless and leering they sit open mouthed
and bemused by the world as it changes
while they just watch and pout

Hope church gargoyles

ESCAPING

From urban dreams of magic his mind soared.
Secret caskets, a manacled hero,
filling the mind of the starstruck child
with secrets and tricks, Randini he'd be

Lines to a master,
the handcuff king,
Houdini the mystifier
replied from his superstar life.
A friendship bound
like the magicians limbs
drawn tight to an attic

A pull on the rope to fly to the roof.
Mother and master looked on below
as Randolph released the buckles of
his trap and the jacket was open.
Shed

A new trick was born that day
to add more pace to the famous art
From Sheffield to the world the tours led out
as the youth looked on

Randolph
Douglas

Then out to the hills his dreams turned
A house of wonder in the castle's lee
Torchlit treasures from far flung lands
In cases of glass trapped like seeds in amber

Tiny models made by the same boy's hands
were mixed with locks and exotic things
Giving others escape to places never seen,
Sending minds on journeys

Then the dust fell on the magic place
Wonder dimmed by age and years
The treasures were scattered to new homes
or lost forever in a musty box

Scrapbooks of tales line fading books,
the master's death, the challenges won.
No words from beyond to cheer
and tell of the greatest return of all

Models in boxes sit on metal shelves
in the museum vault of yellowed light
trapped secrets buried like the man
all waiting for the next escape

STONE DRAGON AT AULT HUCKNALL

For eternity they spar
the little knight and his scaly foe
above the door of the old church.

Trees grow and season pass
snows line the lintel
and sun kisses the warm stones

but still they stand
frozen in time
in the act of jabbing and poking

Bodies filled the ground around them
laid to rest
as they still fight their perpetual battle against each other
and erosion

TRADE MARKS

Like giant's buttons they are
Scattered, heather bound.
Rounded gritstone formed from
angled edge,
bent to a human need
now left and worked by nature.

Millstones never scarred by work,
but worn slowly by time.
Escaping the crushed grain or
knife spark.
Never coughed over by
worn faces of worn men,
never breaking to crush bone
or maim limb.

Redundant they lie.
Murmering of possibilities
not knowing the hands that formed them
have long ago turned to dust.

Abandoned millstones

Leadwort betrays
the hidden depths.
The ore herald.
signal of the grey, sullen prize
sought by groping hands and tools.
Yellow candlelight reflects
in wearying eyes
that see too little sun.
Styx and stones may
break my bones...
or sour my blood...
Bellanded.
Life blighted by the
dark crawlings in
air starved veins.
Men living hardly longer
than a flower.

Leadwort

PADLEY

Scattered stones
lie behind a chapel
risen from the rubble
and called again to praise.
A spiral staircase skeleton
left like a whittled ammonite.
The once proud hall a fossilised blueprint,
now a perch for picnickers.
Struggle and faith's retribution
forgotten in dappled sunlight.

Bees lazily hover
over the ghostly walls.
A door threshold is a racetrack for ants.
What dress once rustled there in haste
to hide the priests,
or pale face watched
through a misted window
for the coming
of the Queen's wrath?

Padley Hall spiral staircase remains

Padley Chapel

Bibliography/further reading

Lime kilns and lime burning
Richard Williams
ISBN 0 -7478-0596 - 2
A shire book outlining the different types of kilns and the history of limeburning

The Gem of The Peak
W. Adam, 1851
A lovely old guide book to the area with some beautiful plate illustrations. Worth looking out for at second hand bookshops. A fascinating glimpse of the tourist industry of the time.

The Cromford Canal
Hugh Potter
ISBN 0-7524--2802-0
A book by the archivist of the Friends of Cromford Canal. and full of information and lots of lovely old photographs. A must have for fans of the canal.

The Book of Edale
The Edale Society
Stories, illustrations, photographs and memories by the people of the village an their community book project

The Peak District at War
Peter Clowes
ISBN 1-897949-76-6
Fascinating insight to lifer during the second world war for the people of the Peak District. Tales of the land army, home guard, evacuees, sad bomber crashes and POWs. Some wonderfully evocative photographs.

Sheffield's Golden Frame. The Moorland Heritage of Burbage, Houndkirk and Longshaw.
Bill Bevan
ISBN 978 1 85058 846 7

Bill Bevan is an archeologist, photographer and writer and has produced a very informative book illustrated with his fine photographs, as well as poems and artwork by local people.

Learn about the archaeology of the area, packhorse routes, its role in World War 2 and more. There are six1 self guided walks too.

A Tour Through England and Wales: Daniel Defoe
(Everyman Library) Originally Published 1724

A wonderful insight to Defoe's contemporary, sometimes moving, sometimes scathing impressions of the Peak and its people

Camden's Britannia:
Wordy late 16th century text that describes the Peak, but fascinating to read

England's Thousand Best Churches
Simon Jenkins
ISBN 0-713-99281-6
Derbyshire/Peak/local ones included are Ashbourne, Ashover, Ault Hucknall, Bakewell, Chesterfield, Steetley, Tideswell Wirksworth and Youlgreave

The Seven Blunders of the Peak, Some Derbyshire Legends Reassessed
Edited by Brian Robinson
ISBN 0-907758-77-0

Tales well known in Derbyshire, such as the Eyam Plague, Little John's grave and Blue John are covered in a new light

View from Houndkirk Road

Murder and Mystery in the Peak
Roly Smith ISBN 1-84114-369-3
Entertaining and interesting accounts of spooky and deadly goings on over the years

Derbyshire Blue John
Trevor D. Ford ISBN 1 87377519 9
Extremely detailed and informative book about the gem

Rocky Rambles in the Peak District
Fred Broadhurst looks at the geology beneath your feet
ISBN 1-8508-750-7

Family Walks in the Peak District and South Yorkshire
John Spenser and Ann Beedham did this illustrated Star Newspaper book of 52 routes graded for ease
ISBN 1 - 85284 257 1

Derbyshire Churchyards
Joyce Critchlow ISBN 0 946404 28 3
Some details to spot, such as sundials and crosses

Prehistory in the Peak
Mark Edmonds and Tim Seaborne ISBN 0 7524 1483 6
Very detailed with very good grid refs, geographic/historical/technical detail in profusion

Bibliography/further reading

Archaeology Walks in The Peak District:
Ali Cooper ISBN 1 850 58 7078
A good way to make history come to life and enjoy a day out

Derbyshire origins A field guide to archeological sites in
North Derbyshire from Sheffield City Museums

Celtic Derbyshire
Peter Naylor ISBN 0 946 404 10 0

Curiosities of the Peak District
Frank Rodgers ISBN 0 903485 47 8
Lots of things to go out and spot that you may have missed

Supernatural Peak District
David Clarke   ISBN 0 7090 6512 4
Journalist and folklorist David Clarke looks at tales of boggarts, phantom planes, black dogs, ghosts etc and talks to people about the strange goings on in the Peak

The Mystery of Carl Wark: Peak District fortress or folly?
Mick Savage ISBN 1 9015 8706 1
Discussion about the enigmatic feature that may or may not be a hill fort

The Iron Age Hillforts of England
Geoffrey Williams   ISBN 1 897817 07 X
Scholarly text full of detail, with Derbyshire s MamTor and Carl Wark included

Collins Gem Guide to Wild Flowers
Marjorie Blamey and Richard Fitter
ISBN 0 00 458 801 0

Collins Gem Guide to Butterflies and Moths
Brian Hargreaves and Michael Chinery
ISBN 0 00 458 808 8
Ideal for sticking in the pocket when wandering around countryside, graveyards etc.

Notable Churches of Derbyshire
Robert Innes Smith
ISBN 0 85 100 072

All About Derbyshire
by Edward Bradbury, 1884.
Simpkin Marshall and Co.
Flowery text as he travels around with his companion Kalmat an rambles on beautifully about blue john etc.

Hidden Derbyshire
Richard Stone ISBN 1 85306 715 6
Some lesser known places to visit and explore

Roman Derbyshire
John J Anderson
Small book about the Roman sites in the area

The Peak District - Landscapes through time
John Barnatt and Ken Smith ISBN 0 77134 7529 3

The Buxton Hydro
Peter Lomas
ISBN 978 1 901214 833
An immensely detailed book about   the history of the town s best known Hydropathic.

The Hard Way Up
Hannah Mitchell s fascinating autobiography.

Rebel Girls
Jill Liddington
ISBN 1 84408 168 0
The tale of how women fought for the right to vote. Including Hannah Mitchell and the Pankhursts.

Backing Into The Limelight
Michael Yardley
ISBN 0245 54 199 3
A biography of T E Lawrence

Twenty Five Years of Play Producing 1927 - 1952
Lawrence Du Garde Peach.
Well worth a read if you can find a copy in a second hand shop or borrow one from a library. It is an entertaining and humourous account of the professional theatre in the village of Great Hucklow and its players.

Maurice by E M Forster
A book inspired by Forster s visit to Edward Carpenter at his home in Millthorpe, near Holmesfield.

The Sheik
E M Hull
Re-published by Virago (ISBN 1 860 401 093 - X)
This is a fun book to read if you can manage to view the outright racism of the time as a thankfully outdated concept, and take it in the context of when it was written. The purple prose and the turns of phrase of the almost masochistic heroine are hard to take seriously now, but at the time were totally shocking.

The House of Wonders
John Lindley
ISBN 978 0 9559251 0 8
25 poems about Randolph Douglas from the Cheshire Poet Laureate 2004. These poems are a sensitive, amusing and insightful homage to the man who lived surrounded by his wonders; an unassuming eccentric who can still inspire us with his sense of wonder and enthusiasm today.
Available from John Lindley at:
www.johnlindley.co.uk or call 01260 273 219

The Secret Life of Houdini
William Kalush and Larry Sloman
ISBN 13: 978 1 8473 9082 0
A wonderful and meticulously researched life of Houdini. Find out just how amazing and driven this famous escapologist was and about his mission to expose fraudulent mediums. The book mentions Castleton s own Randolph Douglas.

England s Last Revolution
John Stevens
ISBN 0 903485 43 5
The story of the revolution in Pentrich in 1817

Wall, heather and view near Houndkirk Road

Useful web addresses and telephone numbers

www.english-heritage.org.uk

www.nationaltrust.org.uk

www.moorsforthefuture.org.uk
A website about the project to restore the Peak District moors damaged by access and recreational pressures.

www.learningcurve.gov.uk
Lots of history notes and information designed for schools and reference. Has details of engineers, textile industry etc

www.pioneers.historians.co.uk
A website with details of many great inventors and engineers, such as Whitworth and Paxton

www.peakdistrictonline.co.uk
Very comprehensive- accommodation to customs, villages, weather, cycling. cricket, childrens activities etc etc

www.peakdistrict-nationalpark.info
All aspects of the peak in this informative site, including geology, wildlife,people, and a virtual guided walk.

On line search facility provides access to reports on biodiversity, archaeology etc.

www.visitderbyshire.co.uk
History, information, famous people, market days, directions

www.picturethepast.org.uk
A site showing historic photos of Derby, Derbyshire, Nottinghamshire and where you can purchase them on line.
Many photos are over 100 years old

Haddon Hall

www.haddonhall.co.uk
The hall's own website

www.chatsworth.org
The Chatsworth website

www.peakmines.co.uk
Website of the Peak District Mining Museum. Matlock Bath

www.showcaves.com
Features the caverns at Castleton

www.peakdistrict.gov.uk
They work towards sustainable development of the Peak District.

High tea. Sheep near Hathersage

■ **Natural England**
Endcliffe, Deepdale Business Park, Ashford Road, Bakewell, Derbys. DE45 1GT
Tel: 01629 816640
e mail: peak.derbys@naturalengland.org.uk
www.naturalengland.org.uk
Great website with lots of information including Lathkill Dale

Peak District National Park Authority
Aldern House Baslow Road, Bakewell, DE45 1AE
Tel: (01629) 816200

■ **Pooles Cavern**
Green Lane Buxton SK17 9DH
Tel: 01298 26978
www.poolescavern.co.uk

Peak District Rangers
■ **email: rangers@peakdistrict.gov.uk**

■ **Pavilion Gardens Buxton**
(01298) 23114
www.paviliongardens.co.uk

■ **Renishaw Hall**
(01246) 432310
www.sitwell.co.uk

■ **Fanshawe Gate Hall**
www.fgh.org.uk

■ **Friends of Cromford Canal**
(0115) 946 4479
www.cromfordcanal.org.uk

■ **Arkwright Society**
(01629) 823256
www.arkwrightsociety.org.uk
www.cromfordmill.co.uk

■ **Cromford Conference Centre**
(01629) 825995

■ **Masson Mills Textile Museum**
www.massonmills.co.uk

■ **Carsington Water Visitor Centre**
(01629) 540696

■ **Buxton Museum and Art Gallery**
Terrace Road, Buxton. (01298) 24658

■ **Peak Cavern**
(01433) 620285
www.devilsarse.com

■ **Speedwell Cavern**
(01433) 620512
www.speedwellcavern.co.uk

■ **Treak Cliff Cavern**
(01433) 620571
www, bluejohnstone.com

■ **Blue John Cavern**
(01433) 620638
www, bluejohn-cavern.co.uk

■ **Fairholmes Visitor Centre**
(01433) 650953.
E.mail: cyclehire@peakdistrict.gov.uk

■ **Bolsover Castle**
■ **Bolsover Cundy House**
(01246) 822844
www.english-heritage.org.uk

■ **The Moorlands Centre**
Fieldhead, Edale, Hope Valley, S33 7ZA
Tel: 01433 670207
e mail: edale@peakdistrict.gov.uk

TOURIST INFORMATION CENTRES

■ **Bakewell**
Tel: (0870) 4447275
Email: bakewell@peakdistrict.gov.uk

■ **Castleton**
(01433) 620679
Email: tourism@peakdistrict.gov.uk

■ **Matlock**
(01629) 583388
Email: matlockinfo@derbyshiredales.gov.uk

■ **Matlock Bath**
(01629) 55082
Email: matlockbathinfo@derbyshiredales.gov.uk

■ **Buxton**
(01629) 25106
e mail: tourism@highpeak.gov.uk
www.visitbuxton.co.uk

Tree topped hill near Rowsley

View from
near the
Grouse Inn

Thanks to:

- Pickard Communication
- The Sheffield Star
- Cath Parker
- Jill Wright
- Trevor Prew
- Nicola Hale
- Ben Hale
- Edward Baker
- Brenda Simpson
- Chris Emmerson
- June Greenwood
- Sir Reresby Sitwell
- Cynthia Ramsden
- Mark Ramsden

- Jim Steinmeyer
- William Kalush
- Prof. E. Dawes
- David Hibberd
- John Lindley
- Hugh Potter
- Christopher Charlton
- Philip Bowler
- Ben Ashmore
- Buxton Museum and Art Gallery
- Barry Richardson
- Professor Brian Robinson
- Peter Harrison
- Florence Nightingale Museum

- Dr. Steve Dumpleton
- Dave Sainty
- Dr. David Clarke
- Alan Walker, Poole's Cavern
- Roger Grayson/Derbyshire Chad
- Manchester Archives
- Sheffield Archives and Information Service

And many other people I have met with or spoken to whilst doing this book. Their help and enthusiasm was most appreciated

Sunset at Longshaw Estate

What life is this if,
full of care, we have
no time to stop
and stare...